ACCOMPLISH IT
7 SIMPLE ACTIONS TO GET THE RIGHT THINGS DONE
AND ACHIEVE YOUR GOALS

By: Mridu Nagrath-Parikh

Editor: Lindsi Solomon
Cover & Book Designer: Raine Digital

ISBN: 9781796548167

Reviews:

This is the book you need to get the right stuff done now. At its core, productivity is really about doing only what matters (while minimizing everything else), and Accomplish It lays out a simple plan to get from A to B lightning fast!

- Jeff Sanders, 5am Miracle

As a wife, mother of three boys, physician, homemaker, health enthusiast, organizational freak and over-achiever, I love to see checkmarks on my daily planner. But, I often feel "busy," "unfocused," and "list - exhausted". If you can relate, Accomplish It will simplify your approach to organization, help you reach your goals, guide you to more efficiently prioritize your time, and redirect your focus to improved productivity. This book needs to be in everyone's home or office!

- Dr. Michelle Goni

As a professional organizer, I didn't think I'd gain much reading Accomplish It but I was wrong! The tips and techniques outlined to create a clear path to productivity while being a very entertaining and engaging read - just what I need to bring new energy into my own business right away.

- Liz Jenkins, A Fresh Space

Accomplish It is one of the most accessible, down to earth books I've seen in a while to help us get out of our own way - and GET STUFF DONE!

- Marcy Strauss Axelrod, Author: On Your Game!

Mridu invites you into her world to learn how to create success and achieve your goals by sharing how SHE did it, too. This book is relatable for anyone who has had a goal they just can't seem to turn into reality, and it makes it EASY to turn that around, once and for all. If reading this book makes you feel like you're getting advice from a friend who cares about your success, it's because she is and she does.

- Kathy Vines, Clever Girl Organizing

Perfect book for a busy mom like me who can be pulled in different directions throughout the day. It helped me focus on how to get more done in a thoughtful pragmatic way!

- Neha Shah

A funny, yet practical, guide to help you take back your time and get more done! Mridu shows you how to avoid distractions, so you can focus on – and complete – what's most important to you.

- Regina D'Alesio, Speaking Strategist

Dedication:

To Viraj, love of my life, thank you for pushing me as no one else would and for your endless patience.

To Vishi, Krishin, Mom, and Papa, you are my inspiration every single day.

TABLE OF CONTENTS

Introduction:
You Can

If you're ready to get control of your time and life, you can.

I don't care how many times you've tried and failed, you can get anything you want when you know how to best use your focus and attention.

It doesn't matter how many times you've shown up late to meetings, *or have forgotten about them completely*, or how many times you got sucked into email and had nothing to show for the day. If you want to take control of your life, you can.

You don't have to be a slave to tweets, chirps, dings, rings, beeps, alerts, emails, meetings, or even that annoying colleague who stops by your desk every five minutes.

You can get through your day, every day, without feeling overwhelmed, scattered, or exhausted.

I'm talking about waking up with a plan, saying "no" without feeling guilty, taking a break from email sans the FOMO, and going for a walk right smack in the middle of your workday. *Apparently, you can take control of your day and break the rules at the same time.*

I'd also like to let you know that you don't have to feel like a loser, failure, or dummy because you haven't figured out how to reach this empowering state of awesomeness all on your own.

Chances are you didn't graduate with a Time Management degree or take a "How to Get Through Your 892 Tasks on Your To-Do List" class in high school. Even if that class existed, it would probably be over complicated and require ten systems just to get it all together.

You're expected to manage yourself, your family, your team, your company, your schedule, your finances, your lists, your relationships, your closet, your inventory, your meals, your transportation, your hygiene, your health, and your receipts *this one still gets me tripped up...* and yet you go through 18 years of education without ever taking a single class on managing anything at all.

I'm here to tell you good news has arrived, and it is that you, Almighty Scattered and Reactive One, have everything inside of you to put an end to feeling powerless and to start making the impact you know you are capable of.

All you need to do is wake up to the patterns that are holding you back, make compelling new choices, and consistently implement small but powerful tweaks.

This is what you will learn from this book.

I personally transformed my business and life from a place of stagnancy *just treading water* to one of prosperity, success, and ease, and I believe that you can to.

If I can do it, I know you can.

I went from...

- ...just barely breaking even to busting through new financial levels.

- …complaining about brain fog to meditating daily.

- ...unhappy with my love handles to losing fifteen pounds.

- ...unmotivated to get out of bed to reaching "morning person" status.

Seriously. Who Am I?

Best of all, my plummeted confidence steadily climbed up the self-esteem ladder, simply by feeling successful about what I was doing and knowing where my time was going. What I've learned through my journey is that feeling "in control" is awesome, motivating, and looks pretty good in a pair of skinny jeans. *Who doesn't want to look good in a pair of skinny jeans for crying out loud?*

This is where I give you my "If I can do it, you can too" speech. Because it really is true.

Let me admit it from the beginning, I had no business ever getting into business. I had no idea how to focus on what mattered most in my biz. You know, things like sales, growth, and paying rent. *Not to mention how to make a real impact in the world.*

I spent years drowning in self-sabotaging mindsets, habits, and behaviors that put other people's needs ahead of mine, when I should have been getting in alignment with what would help me reach my goals.

I spent most of the time as an entrepreneur in denial of what really needed to be done. I thought if I worked harder, complained more about how hard I was working, and stayed busy, busy, busy, that eventually, all my hard work would pay off. *Right?!...Wrong.*

My foolproof plan to get out of the busyness and into a real business was to hire more coaches, invest in more technology, and read more marketing books. Not to say those tools weren't helpful, but none of them addressed the real problem.

I was perpetually overwhelmed, unfocused, and I had lost sight of what it meant to truly feel successful at the end of each day. The truth is, I excelled at mediocrity.

I was a champ at staying busy, at doing all the things, at checking tasks off the list, and even adding them to my list after I'd done them just so I could see them checked off. *I know, I'm sly like that.*

I was Queen of feeding my instant gratification addiction with never-ending emails, alerts, and texts. *Give me more, more, more!*

Below the surface, there was a lurking sense of failure, which slowly and steadily chipped away at my confidence. My goals were big, but my progress was small.

Here's the kicker...on the outside, I looked like I had it all together. The real deal. The bee's knees. The Life Is Organized lady! ...*that was on the outside.*

It was not because I was dumb or uneducated. Looking back, it was a combination of being unaware and doubtful. I was unaware of many of the lessons and strategies I'm going to share with you in this book and doubtful about the fact that things could be so simple.

If it were so simple to not feel overwhelmed and get more done than ever, then why wouldn't everyone be doing it? I just knew it had to be more difficult.

Before we jump into new ways of empowering yourself here is lesson #1. Word of caution: It might throw you off your rocker.

Drum roll, please...

Taking control of your time and life isn't complicated.

I'll say it again, read it slower this time:

Taking. Control. Of. Your. Time. And. Life. Is. Not. Complicated.

You don't need binders full of blog posts or 27 hours of YouTube instruction to get you on track. The tips and tools I share are simple – but, as we both know, simple isn't always easy to do. It requires you to strip away your old, cozy habits and replace them with uncomfortable ones that conform after a dozen wears.

This may take some time to sink in. You will want to make this harder than it is. I know it well. I was stuck in that cycle for years. Where are the 18-step processes and 12-page flowcharts to create my schedules and track my behaviors? I need more acronyms!

This book will challenge you to simplify your thinking and simplify your life. Here's what else you'll learn in this book.

Work-life balance is a big fat lie! … *at least in my world*. I like to refer to it as: "work-life integration", "work-life imbalance", or how about just – "life"?

If you can't get out of your house in the morning on time, with two matching shoes, and with confidence that *all* your children are in the backseat, you're certainly not going to kill it in your 9:00 am client presentation.

It's challenging and unrealistic to compartmentalize your life between work and home. If your kid is sick or your toilet is clogged, you can't push the "off" button on those thoughts until 5:00 pm. The lines between professional and personal life are increasingly blurred given our 24/7 connectivity to rising expectations in the home, with our family, and at work.

Being an entrepreneur, I deal with this every day. *I actually had much better luck at managing my time when I had a corporate job.* You'll see that this book is written from my perspective of managing things with <u>my business</u> *and* <u>with my family.</u>

Which is why I'll share examples of sales funnels to laundry systems because, at the end of the day, the strategies to manage your time are the same. It's simply the environment that is different.

You might need to read that one again. The strategies to manage your time are the same. It's the environment that is different. *More on that in just a bit...*

When I started my career, I organized photos and videos. I loved telling people's stories through the pages of creative photo books and whimsical video montages that chronicled everything from their ice cream escapades, to their fascinating eight decades of life. As I worked closely with people on their most personal memories, they invited me to take a look at their storage closets or pantries for organizing tips too.

Organizing was a gift that came to me naturally, so I thought I'd love tearing apart people's laundry rooms and garages. However, it didn't take me long to realize that...well...I didn't. It was a lot more fun to ponder over my own set of barely used bicycle shorts *just in case I ever buy a bike* than it was to help others decide if their sequined pants from 1983 were more likely to come back in fashion. *Unless it's for New Year's Eve, I really hope not.*

I loved my clients, but I wasn't fulfilled with my role. I felt like people were **leaning** on me versus **learning** from me, as I was organizing for them and not teaching them the skills they needed to succeed on their own.

It was around this period of uncertainty that I was introduced to the online world of courses and workshops. I took a class on building a website to get more local traffic. My instructor was in Ohio and I was in Nashville. We met twice a month over conference calls, and she emailed her members downloads, videos, and homework.

Mind. Blown. I could learn marketing skills without ever meeting my teacher or leaving my living room, sitting in my pajamas, and sipping on wine. *Perhaps it was the sipping on wine part that really got me most excited about offering this type of education?* Still, I knew this was how I wanted to build my business. Nine months later, I give birth to my third *and very colicky* child, "Life Is Organized." (www.lifeisorganized.com).

Within a year, I mastered my branding, created an award-winning suite of home organization online courses and workshops, and was raking in the cash. I was well on my way to a six-figure business.

Baaahahahahahaha. That was a good one, wasn't it?

It was more like I was investing startling amounts of money I didn't have, launching and scrapping business models I didn't have a clue about, and pulling my hair out learning code for the back end of my infuriating site without a smidge of technology background.

In fact, I was so raw that when I started thinking about my online venture, my husband suggested I start a "blog". I embarrassingly can admit that I responded...*wait for it...wait for it...*

"What's a "blog"??"

Yes, sweet friend. I was *that* clueless.

Fast-forward through a very challenging and grueling three years. I poured my heart and soul into my business, investing countless hours, day, weeks, months, obsessing over my content, blogs, videos, e-courses, marketing, and training. I devoured every book on business development, entrepreneurship, personal growth, mindset, sales, promotion, and branding.

Through all this inspiration and knowledge, I knew that if I just put my head down, if I just made the sacrifices, if I just did put in the time – I would succeed.

One Saturday afternoon I waved goodbye to my family, my hubby and two sons, ages 7 and 10, as they were off to a birthday party that I was missing because I was working so hard. I was just so busy. The next morning my husband walked into my office and said those four little words that never bode well for a good conversation. *"We need to talk."* What followed threw me into an emotional tizzy.

"So… (insert dramatic pause) …when are you going to turn this hobby into a business?"

Did he just call my BUSINESS a "Hobby" …!?

Before I could lunge across the room and punch him in the face, this deep hard lump formed in my throat and waterfalls poured down my face. I somehow mustered up my voice enough to belt out: *"This IS a business. Can't you see how hard I'm working?! Plus, I'm juggling the kids and the house and the projects and the travel. Can't you see how many hours I'm putting in?!"*

"But what about the sales, honey?"

….

I didn't talk to him for a day or two after that. *I'm a big baby like that.* It was a reality check for me.

How was I not making the impact I knew I was capable of?

Why was I not getting to my goals fast enough?

…and for goodness sake

Where was all my time going?

Many months of shifting my perspective, retraining my brain, and adopting new habits, resulted in significant changes to how I now spend my time. Intentionally using my time has had a powerful impact on my life, my family, my health, and my now a financially and personally rewarding business.

This self-realization is what I'm here to teach you in this book because I know that you can take control of your time too...and guess what? You, too, can get anything you want.

If your goal is to grow a business, get a promotion, lose 20 pounds, be a better mom, meet the love of your life, write a book, or buy a house - you can reach your goal, you can have the success you want, in any area you want, when you intentionally take control of where your time goes.

I realize I needed to teach the very thing I was lacking. How to truly be successful by getting the right things done.

It was then that I transitioned my business from helping others to reach their goals at home, to reaching their goals at work. As I switched from home organizing to work productivity, I often got asked how I learned these efficient strategies and tools without training or certification. Well, here's the secret I learned along my journey. *You already read it a few pages back.*

I didn't need to learn any new strategies because whether it's your Outlook calendar at work or your paper planner at home, whether it's creating a process for your marketing assistant or a process for your babysitter, whether it's reaching your professional goals or reaching your personal goals, the strategies are the same. It's the environment that is different.

- If you can organize your closet, you can organize your workspace.

- If you can be punctual to your doctor's appointment, you can be punctual for a team meeting.

- If you can find the time to watch Breaking Bad, you can find the time to get to the gym.

On the flipside,

- If you can't say "Now's not a good time." when your friend calls in the middle of your workday, you won't be able to have a conversation with a client about prioritizing their projects.

- If you can't control your social media habit for one meal with your family, you won't be able to keep focused for 20 minutes on your proposal.

- If you can't prioritize exercise in the morning, you won't prioritize creating that new training program that doesn't have a deadline either.

As you read through each Chapter, ask yourself how you can apply what you're learning to your home, to your family, to your business, or even your volunteer group. The strategies work in every part of your life.

One last note about this book. It is not about perfection, or always getting it right, or never feeling overwhelmed.

It does, however, give you the easy-peasy strategies to set you up for success and give you the tools to fall back on when you *do* feel anxious and stressed out.

I'll let you in on some classified information. I feel overwhelmed all the time.

I have days that I overcommit.

I have days that I procrastinate.

I have days that I feel uninspired.

I have days that I waste on social media.

Sweet friend, I have those days, but I now know HOW to get myself out of these emotionally unfulfilling cycles and into a sequence of motivating actions that improve my outcomes and ultimately, make me happier.

I like happy. Happy is good. If you like happy, you'll like this book.

Getting a handle on your time isn't about cramming in "more, more, more" in fewer hours. It's about giving yourself the freedom to be and do whatever makes you feel successful instead of acting like a victim to everyone else's demands.

It's about creating the freedom and space to live the life you were meant to live. We all have the power within us to choose how and when we spend our time.

I knew I wanted to do big things, be a better role model, make an impact on my work, and stop feeling behind all the time. If I'd put the same amount of energy and focus that I did into procrastinating, perfecting, prolonging, pretending, and processing, into getting the meaningful things done, I'd be reaching my goals years before I actually did.

We see people everywhere controlled by their circumstances. *"One more meeting this week and I might explode!"*

We hear them whine about never having enough time. *"I can't get to the gym, I'm soooo busy!"*

We watch them make excuses. *"With my schedule, who has time to volunteer?"*

Being busy has become a badge of honor. You pin it to your shirt so everyone (including yourself) knows how hard you're working, how important you are, and how much you're getting done. Like there's a prize behind curtain #3 awarded to the Busiest Bee of all.

Add that to your ever-distracted demeanor, reacting to beeps, dings, and rings; giving them undue urgency and immediate responses.

Even though I teach this stuff, I fall into the same traps too. I find myself getting distracted so easily that it means failing to finish projects, neglecting relationships, and avoiding my priorities. I've even told my kids I was working when it was time to put them to bed when really, I was perusing the latest Presidential scandal. *I know. It's a sickness.*

Distractions are everywhere. We have our email open. Our phones are on the desk next to us. There are 37 tabs open on our laptop and sometimes right in the middle of reviewing our Google stats we'll think of something and start researching, or order a book on Amazon, or look at plane tickets. Like, right in the middle of another totally unrelated thought.

We usually don't even notice when we pick up the phone and check Facebook. It's a reflex. An involuntary impulse like breathing or chewing. *Wait, did I just pick up my phone eight times while we were talking? Sorry, it's out of my control. It just happens.*

Distractions are the biggest enemies of our focus and concentration. They. Are. Ruthless. They keep on coming without a second thought about how they're affecting us. How they're tearing us away from doing the things that matter most. They have no remorse for their offensive behavior, no matter how far and how long they've strayed us from what we know what we really should be doing. They steal our presence with our friends, kids, and colleagues. They strip of us traits we used to cherish like focus, attention, and good old-fashioned eye contact. They even seem to multiply the more we give in to them.

I'll quickly check my email, and the first one tells me I need to check into my flight, which reminds me I need to buy *sun*block, then it hits me that I didn't sign the permission slip for my *son*, which causes me to upload his spring concert pics on Facebook, which flashes an ad on the perfect yoga pants, which takes me to their website, but I bet I can search for a better price on Amazon, which reminds me to order the push pins in my shopping cart, which sends me a tracking message, guess where?... back in my email!

It's up to us to take the distractions by the horns and show them who's in charge. We can't just assume because we say we'll get our writing done (or whatever our goal is) that we won't fall prey to interruptions.

I could suggest turning off all notifications, deleting your Facebook account, and extracting yourself from all social contact, but you'd probably stop reading right about...now. *Don't go! I won't tell you to do that...*

Instead, I'll tell you about easy-peasy ways to plan for them carefully...remember this is actually quite simple and set up barriers to prevent them from raining on your focus parade.

We'll spend the most time on this topic (Chapter One) because I believe if you did nothing else other than eliminate your distractions, you would reach productivity guru status. You would discover time you lost along the way, get clarity you never knew existed, and radically squash your scatteredness.

As you stop operating from a place of overwhelm, (a remarkable by-product of increased clarity and understanding what's most important), you can see what you need to do, and you can also see that you are making progress. Which attracts my favorite four-syllable word into life: Mo-ti-va-tion.

When you feel good about what you are accomplishing, when you achieve what you set out to do, when you think, "Dayum, I got so much done today!" you have fewer snarky remarks for your kiddos, are less irritated by your hubby's dishes on the coffee table, and wake up the next morning inspired to kick even more ass than yesterday.

<u>Bottom line: When you feel good, you do good.</u>

There was no one a-ha moment for when I finally figured out how to take control of time, – or get clear of what I really wanted, but rather a culmination of feeling overworked, overcommitted, overwhelmed and simply, over it.

I just finally started making small changes, tweaks really, and the magic dust sprinkled over my life improving what I was accomplishing and how I was feeling.

"You mean if I focus for thirty minutes, I could take care of all these bills instead of them lingering over me for two weeks?" "This. Is. Genius."

"Is it possible that if I planned ahead of time, I would know exactly what I was working on for the day?" "Where have you been all my life?!"

"Can it be that if I wrote down the specialty latte flavor at Starbucks this morning, I could remember it three months from now?" "This is simply too much to take in."

With each small habit change, I began to see a powerful impact on my business, relationships, health, and income. I laid one tiny time or energy boosting brick at a time, simultaneously building my confidence and results.

It does take practice, it does take consistency... but it doesn't take anything else that you don't already have inside of you.

Instead of clinging to how you're used to doing things, open your heart and mind to embracing a new way of thinking and free yourself of imprisoning thoughts like "but that's what everybody's doing."

Have faith there is a better way. Have belief you are capable of more. Have strength in your desire to end each day feeling successful.

I could never have built my coaching program, gotten incredible results, made time for my family, reached my weight goal, or shifted back to spirituality, without honing my focus, prioritizing what was most important, and shutting out the chatter that had been holding me back for years.

No matter how scary each step was, it was nowhere near as frustrating as the feeling of failure or perpetual "meh" I was living in. It's exciting to know I have a roadmap for my goals, a guidance for my days, and am moving the big fat needle towards my professional and personal targets every day. *Well almost. Friendly reminder: I have off days too.*

I want you to know that you have everything you need right now to start turning your overwhelmed reality into a well-oiled machine that leaves you feeling successful, confident, and happy each day.

We've been raised to believe that the harder you work, the more successful you'll be, but the truth is you simply need to work smarter, get comfortable with the uncomfortable, and stick with the tools and strategies repeatedly, especially when you fall off.

You must not only commit to allowing freedom, you must give yourself permission to do so. Every time I start coaching a new client about reaching their goals or taking control of their time, I hear the uncertainty in their voice. I always reassure them it's supposed to feel a little scary and a little exciting, at the same time.

If you didn't have a sliver of doubt or fear, you wouldn't be growing. You'd be doing things the same way you'd been doing them for months and years. *...And look where that's gotten us.*

If you're ready for things to be different you've got to do different. It's the thrilling discomfort of knowing that on the other side of the uneasiness, things will be better. They will be easier. You will be happier.

There will even come a time when you'll think, *"Why didn't I try this earlier?"*

My hope for you is that you read this book over and over, and you do what it says. Pick a strategy, work at it, fail at it, tweak it, get back to it, try it again, master it and then move on to the next.

You'll know which one speaks to you best, as I introduce one key strategy in each chapter because it will be exactly the one you need to hear most right now, wherever you are in your journey to take control of your life.

The tools you need are all waiting for you right here, right now. Dive in, have fun and get on the path to getting the right things done. I'll see you on the other...accomplished side.

Chapter One:
Why You Stay In Stuckness

(Code Letter: "A")

My son has a superpower.

We didn't know what to do with his paranormal ability when he was a child. At first, we were in awe. "Look what he can do!" As his power grew, though, from infrequent intrigue to superhuman endurance, we wondered how he would apply it in the world.

Would he use it for good? Would he use it for evil? Would he harness his ability to create a universe of other superhumans, or would he destroy our entire existence?

I'm not going to lie. As parents, we had concerns about his misalignment with other kids his age. Something was a little off. A little different. A little extraordinary.

He isn't faster than a speeding bullet or stronger than a zooming train. In today's world of digital addiction and ubiquitous connectivity, his gift is even more powerful.

That boy can focus like nobody's business.

Who cares if all the kids are playing in the be-all end-all freeze tag tournament, determining their coolness rank across the entire first grade?

Who cares if the Eagles are about to win their first Super Bowl – ever?

Is that smoke in the house? Oh well. I'll just keep my head down and keep doing what I'm doing. ...*Mom and Dad will take care of it.*

Seriously, he can focus to the point where if we didn't pull him out of his room and force him to eat and shower, he'd walk in there a young boy and walk out years later, a young adult. *With really bad body odor.*

When he decides he's going to do or learn something, he means it. With raw, real, concrete, unstoppable conviction. With "nothing else matters until I master this" chutzpah. With "why wouldn't I go all in? It doesn't make sense to do it any other way."

For a kid who rolls his eyes at all things 80's, (could anything be more uncool?), I couldn't imagine that the six-sided puzzle would revolutionize his world. I don't remember his introduction to The Rubik's Cube, but the challenge sparked his curiosity and ignited his superpower almost immediately.

For the next few months, he incessantly poured over YouTube videos. At first, he wanted to simply learn the solve; a goal that would satisfy most typical humans.

But for my son, the solve was a rite of passage, a simple token of baseline interest. He quickly transitioned to mastering the speed of the solve. I'm not talking doing it under three minutes, which would be jaw-dropping for me. I'm talking, twelve second solves, which was regarded as normal for "Cubers." *Yes, twelve seconds... I told you. Super. Powers.*

Algorithm after algorithm after algorithm, he memorized permutations, researched speed cubes, and obsessed over timing his solves.

Everywhere we looked he had cubes. Under his pillow, on his desk, and in his backpack. They were always in his hands. He mastered one handed solves, solving two cubes at one time, and even solving cubes underwater while holding his breath.

He competed in Cube competitions where he traded computational shortcuts so he could shave off a second here and a second there. A twenty-second solve was no longer acceptable. He had to get better. With his superpower, there was no stopping him from getting what he wanted.

That boy can focus like nobody's business.

He eats, dreams, and breathes the skill he wants to learn or improve. I call it obsessive, but at the back of my mind I'm always thinking: "How can I get more of that?"

For most of us "normal type", staying focused is really freakin' hard.

It's hard to walk from your kitchen to your bedroom without getting distracted.
It's challenging to plan your day without getting sucked into your email.
It's nearly impossible to post a Facebook update without perusing your friends' latest accolades or love for their spouse. *Really? You can't do this face-to-face?*

We are connected twenty-four seven.

That smartphone is no longer an accessory, but an extension of our limbs. We wake up to it by our bedside, blowing up with alerts, updates, and so-called emergencies. We scroll through social media hour by hour, often minute by minute.

According to research in the journal "Social Psychology", even if you go all day without touching your cell phone once, *like that's ever going to happen,* just having it in sight, distracts you from completing your tasks.

Why are we so addicted to our phones, laptops, and iPads? Do we simply not have any self-control? Are we that powerless against our electronics?

The truth is, with every response to a text, tweet, email, ding, beep, alert, chirp, and notification, you get a dopamine hit, (this controls the "pleasure" systems of the brain), making you feel pure enjoyment, which motivates you to want more, more, more!

It's like a party going on in your brain. And every time you react or respond to a distraction you get rewarded with a shot of the party drug, which further addicts you to this behavior.

You know how great it feels to be the first one to respond to a group chat, or how awesome it has felt to reply to a text within seconds, and just how sweet it is to kick off the comments on your niece's communion photos.

Damn you, dopamine!

Let me ask you this, do you feel happy at the end of the day when you know you spent a good part of it scrolling through Facebook, Instagram, and email, when the stuff you really should have been focusing on feels even heavier now?

I know I don't. I feel guilty because I wasted my day with something that doesn't add a lot of value to my day.

What does add value and make me happy?

For me, it is going to bed knowing I was productive and realizing that I am one step closer to my goals. In other words, I must get things done that really matter to me (exercise, make sales calls, spend time with my boys) to feel good and accomplished at the end of the day.

The plethora of gadgets and social tools that were meant to increase productivity are now the biggest enemy of our focus. We willingly allow them to invade our concentration, drastically lower our efficiency, and bring on a whole lotta unnecessary stress into our lives.

Let's talk about how these focus stealers affect our behavior. Does this sound familiar?

It's Monday morning, 9:00 a.m., and I am ready to start my day and get cracking at my to-do's. Right after I grab a cup of coffee. While that's heating up, I'll just throw these dishes in the dishwasher. The disposal sounds wonky. Maybe a plastic spoon is caught in there? That reminds me that when the spoon hit my tooth this morning, it stung. I should call the dentist. I grab my phone to auto-dial and ding, ding, ding...3 new texts. Mom needs to ask me a question, a client asks if I have a second, and my bestie sends me a link to Coldplay's new song. When I click on the song link ...*because clearly, this is the most urgent task I need to attend to right now* an ad pops up for the Banana Republic sweater I had just clicked on last night. I should get it while the sale is on. I'll do it right now before I forget.

As I'm checking out I get an alert from "The Skimm" about today's breaking news, and as I click on that, I realize I need my credit card for the BR transaction, which is my wallet upstairs. I start walking and see my son's sweatshirt, belt, and jersey are strewn across the floor. *So annoying!* I'll just grab this stuff and throw it in his room. I open the door and see the fish tank. Did he feed them? I'll just send him a quick text to find out.

I hit my head on the side of the door as I'm walking into my office, head down, typing away. I sit down at my desk and see I have 27 unread emails from within the last two hours. My heart simultaneously sinks and skips a beat when I see one from a prospect I've been waiting to hear back from for weeks. I'm about to dive in as I reach for my mug and I realize: Wait. Where's my coffee?

Seriously? What. Is. Wrong. With. Me?!!

Our monkey minds seem to get more distracted every day. Plus, we can no longer compartmentalize work and home. The boundaries between our professional and personal lives are blurring, which further complicates our ability to get and stay focused.

Work on the strategy.
Call the doctor.
Pay the bills.
Create the social media plan.
Follow up with the painter.
Instruct the coach.

Facilitate the meeting.
Pick up the dry cleaning.
Hire the assistant.
Plan the meals.
Post the blog.
Make the grocery list.
Analyze the results.

We are constantly distracted by demands, to-dos, and decisions. This barrage of information, ideas and thoughts, stretches our time and energy, leaving us feeling scattered and unsuccessful.

It's no fun working, working, working from morning till night, doing all things, checking them off your list, always being "on", yet end up feeling unfulfilled at the end of the day.

How can we stop this insanity? This constant battle between what needs to get done and what you actually do given the distractions that stand smack in the middle of your path.

Here's the bottom line. You have got to bring it back to the basics and do the simple stuff.

The stuff you *know* you should be doing but don't.
The stuff you *know* you should be focusing on but can't.
The stuff you *know* you should be dealing with but won't.

The stuff that leaves you feeling happy and successful before you lay your head down each night. The things that make your day fulfilling and your life rewarding.

Multitasking makes you stupid

Like many ambitious people, you probably take great pride in being a multitasker. You send email, talk on your phone, check the market, and take meeting notes all at the same time *...or so you think*. As a multitasking expert, you believe the more you react to, the more productive you are.

As the official bubble buster around here, it's my job to tell you that on the contrary, multitasking makes you lousy at getting anything done efficiently or effectively. That's because your brain has limited energy each day.

The more you switch tasks, the more you zap the energy out of it, which makes you do things like send an email without the attachment, forget your client's name, or suffer from general brain fog by early afternoon.

The best analogy I can make to your brain and its counterproductive information overload is to your cell phone. You charge your phone at night and in the morning it's fully charged, and the battery is green.

Over the course of the day you check Facebook, jump onto Amazon, watch a YouTube video, check Instagram, respond to eight texts, take three calls, create a Pinterest board, Waze the directions, check the weather, post on Twitter, read a few articles, share a video, and so on and so on. Then, before you know it, let's say by 3:00 p.m., your battery is red, you're almost out of power, and you need to recharge your phone again.

Your brain is the same way.

You wake up in the morning, fully charged and battery full. Over the course of the day you incessantly jump back and forth from text, to call, to search, to post, to spreadsheet, to list, to document, to conversation, to email, to plan, to response, to thought, to worry, to article, to video, to news, and so on and so on. Then, like clockwork, let's say by 3pm, your brain is fried, your energy is spent, your battery is red, you're just about out of power and need to recharge again.

Each time you jump to another thought or activity, *hello multitasking*, and get back to what you were working on just before you got distracted, you invest brain power in reprocessing information. What a waste of your reservoir of energy in your battery power! You chip away at your battery life faster and faster each time you switch thoughts.

Neuroscience research tells us that the brain doesn't really do tasks simultaneously, as we thought *or hoped* it might. In fact, we just switch tasks quickly. Each time we move from hearing music to writing a text to talking to someone, there is a stop/start process that goes on in our brain.

Rather than saving time, that start/stop/start process *costs* time (even very small microseconds), it's less efficient, and we make more mistakes. There is a lag time during which your brain must yank itself from the initial task and get into the new task. This shift, though it feels instantaneous, takes time. In fact, up to 40 percent more time than single tasking (focusing on one task at a time) - especially for complex tasks.

Yup, you read that right. You can waste up to 40% of your day by constantly switching between tasks. *FORTY. PERCENT!*

I don't know about you, but instead of feeling behind and scattered, I'd rather take those few hours every day to get other important tasks done, leave work early, exercise, spend time with my family, watch Game of Thrones, or simply do my current work better and without feeling so overwhelmed.

If you're into easy...

On the next few pages, there are six ways you can avoid the distractions, squash the multi-tasking, make daily progress on your goals and feel really good about what you get done at the end of each day.

Spoiler alert! These strategies are simple. So simple you may have the initial tendency to think "This is too easy!", or "I've tried that, and it didn't work!", or "I've read/heard about that, really what is the big deal?"

The deal is this. They work. Yes, they are easy, but sometimes the easiest things are the ones we don't do or choose to overlook.

Keep an open mind. Don't start this book or begin another day from a place of self-sabotage.

I've spoken across the country, implemented these strategies with thousands of ambitious people like you and continue to receive emails and testimonials about their success. This stuff works. Let's put it into action.

Before we jump into the easy-peasy solutions, allow me to sum up your biggest challenge when it comes to distractions. You, my sweet friend, rely on willpower.

Let me tell you something about willpower - *it sucks!*

Whether you want to get healthier, cut down on using social media, improve your relationships, write a book, or grow your business--willpower alone won't help you achieve any of these goals.

Remember, when it comes to social and technological distractions we're talking about neural addictions. If you're serious about the changes you want to make, willpower won't be enough. In fact, it's the opposite. Willpower is what's holding you back.

According to psychological research, your willpower is like a muscle. It's a finite resource that depletes with use. As a result, by the end of your day, your willpower muscles are exhausted, and you're left to your defenseless self, with almost zero control to stop the time wasters.

Instead of relying on willpower, your best bet is to eliminate your distractions completely. Out of sight and out of mind is a real thing.

I'm not suggesting you throw your phone out the window or delete all your social media accounts ...*although I bet that would be super healthy for you*. However, there are simple and less intrusive ways to eliminate the temptations without depending on willpower ...and feeling like a failure at the end of each day.

Are you ready for these life-changing strategies? Let's go!

Number One: Clear your desk.
If you're already rolling your eyes, remember your promise to be open-minded. This may or may not sound like an obvious one but either way, let me break it down for you.

Distractions are anything that prevents you from giving your full attention to something else. Which means when you see stuff, on your desk, in front of you, or in your peripheral view, your brain does a quick processing, *it's smart like that*, and breaks your concentration. Don't let the fact that you don't always recognize it, make you believe it's not happening.

Here's typically what happens. You sit down to write a proposal and you're getting deep into thought, otherwise known as "a flow". Otherwise known as "concentration". Otherwise known as "doing your best work".

As you're thinking of the next step or strategy to outline, your eyes shift. Looking up is a sign of thinking. When you look up and see the invoice that needs to be paid, or the sticky note with "call Laura" or the trash that needs to be picked up; your natural tendency is to process that information and get momentarily, if not temporarily, distracted. You may grab that piece of paper, folder, or dirty napkin in an effort to be more productive.

"Let me take care of this now before I forget."
"It would be super exciting to cross this off my to-do list, and even more exciting if it wasn't on my to-do list, I did it, and then I went back to my list just to add it in and cross it off."

I know your type because I've done this one too many times myself.

Even if you don't physically take action on what interrupts your flow, it is going on your mental checklist, isn't it?

Call the plumber.
Mail the check.
Read the book.
Update the post.
Correct the number.
Increase the touchpoints.

Simply seeing it adds it to your ever-growing list, whether you know you're doing this or not.

This is why clearing your desk *or whatever space you're working in* is so valuable in keeping you on task.

Important Note #1: Clearing your desk does not give you permission to spend the next two hours organizing your papers and files, creating labels and color coordinating folders. Do not use this tip as a procrastination technique for getting your work done. You're pretty sly like that, but as a serial procrastinator, I'm calling you out on it. Just take the stuff off your desk. Easy-peasy.

Important Note #2: Clearing your desk also does not mean putting everything in a big pile to the side of you. Take the folders, stickies, papers, magazines, books, and other random stuff and simply put it behind you on the floor or on a table. Create elbow room so you're comfortable and get all the stuff out of your peripheral view too, which is equally distracting as what's directly in front of you. Do not rely on willpower.

Important Note #3: The ONE thing you should leave on your desk is a pad of paper. Guess when the most ideas and thoughts are going to come to you? When you're trying to focus! It's kind of like meditating. Instead of acting on those thoughts, (email Betsy, follow up with Roger, water the plants), you want to have a convenient place to capture them so you can act on them later. The key word here is *later*. Not while you're doing your best to focus. Writing your thoughts as they come to you gives you the peace of mind that you won't lose them and that they won't fall through the cracks. Also, if you keep your running to-do list on a digital source, (I use and love Evernote), you can skip the paper and keep that ONE tab open. Otherwise, no other exceptions.

Easy enough, right? YES. Let's move onto distraction avoidance strategy #2.

Number Two: Turn off the notifications.
Fo' real, sister.

Doesn't it feel great to be super responsive? So gratifying to send an immediate "yes!" to your client about that meeting, Be the first to report on your favorite movie in that Facebook group, or to "like" that tweet immediately after you get an alert about it.

If this is you, consider yourself a UJ: An Urgency Junkie.

Urgency Junkies are driven, ambitious and overall go-getters. That's exactly why UJ's like you react the moment you receive an email or a response to your latest post or tweet.

Urgency Addict, you need to stop this behavior. Put an end to the constant reactiveness to every text, message, beep, ding, or alert you hear or see.

TRUTH BOMB: IT IS A TOTAL PRODUCTIVITY BUZZKILL.

Research shows that we receive at least one email every four minutes and one other notification (like a text or tweet) every three minutes. Feeling the need to react tears you away from your current focus. *Yes, just reading the email or text counts.*

Plus, think about this. Everyone is busy. Do they really need to hear from you as imperatively as you think they do?

Uh…NO.

If you're struggling with:
- not getting enough of the important work done all day
- getting buried in emails and texts
- always feeling distracted and scattered…

…. PUH-LEASE, for the love of all things efficient, turn off ALL your notifications.

THOSE LITTLE BUGGERS ARE RUINING YOUR ABILITY TO GET ANYTHING DONE AND TO REACH YOUR FULL POTENTIAL.

Remember that party going on in your brain every time you react or respond to a distraction? You get rewarded with a shot of the party drug, which addicts you to this behavior.

So, good news – your addiction to reacting is not your fault.

Bad news – keeping your notifications on – is.

If turning off alerts from email, social media, news and anywhere else that is distracting you, is giving you heart palpitations – Relax.

Instead of living in constant reaction mode, block out time on your schedule throughout the day to check on these very tasks. Like:

- Block 10 minutes at the end of each hour to respond to your texts and tweets
- Block 15 minutes to respond to emails AFTER you've focused on a task for 40 minutes
- Block 30 - 60-minute increments to check and respond to email three times a day (the rest of the day your email tab is closed!)

We'll get a lot more into how to block your time effectively in Chapter Three.

Beyond staying focused, other powerful benefits to kicking those little notification buggers to the curb are:
- **Higher energy**: you'll see a significant increase in energy level when your brain power doesn't get sucked throughout the day.
- **More time**: look forward to saving at least an hour in your day (to get the same stuff done that you were before).
- **Better results**: reach your goals faster, with more clarity and quality.

Will it be scary to turn off your notifications?

Of course, it will!

Every change from your norm feels uneasy at first, but no change will come from doing things like you've always done them. So...

Take a small but mighty step outside your comfort zone. Have faith in your ability to eliminate distractions that are holding you back and have the courage to turn off those little notification buggers. *You will thank yourself later.*

Number Three: Close the tabs.

Give me a virtual fist bump if you have 47 tabs open on your laptop right now. Yeah, I thought as much.

I know, I know. You don't want to forget to read that article, print that recipe, or update that web page. So, leave the tabs open because that's the perfect way to stay focused and get everything done. *Isn't it cute how we convince ourselves of these ideas?*

I've got breaking news for you. Just as the papers, folder, stickies, invoices, articles, and magazines on your desk break your concentration, so do the tabs open on your screen. Except the tabs are even more dangerous as they loom over you and are a constant reminder of everything you *haven't* gotten done.

Brace yourself. If you are ready to play at a higher level, feel in control and magnify your focus superpower, you need to close them.

You heard me. Close them. All of them. Especially the email tab. The only tabs that should stay open are the ones related to the ONE task you're working on. Here's an insanely simple example *...in case you didn't catch onto the theme here.*

Working on your finances? Keep your FreshBooks tab open and your bank account tab open. Close Facebook, LinkedIn, Email, Pinterest, Articles You're Reading, Recipes, Digital Classes, and everything else that doesn't have to do with your finances.

You will instantly gain clarity. When your beautiful eyes shift up on the screen, as of course, they will when you're thinking, you'll see nothing but what you're working on.

You won't have to rely on willpower to *not* click on any of the 72 other tabs you have open.
Your mind won't fret with everything you still have to get done.
Your eyes won't shudder back and forth across your screen with anxiety.

Your immediate thought may be: "How will I remember everything I need to do if I don't keep at least 54 tabs in sight at all times?"

I've got three words for you. Paper and Bookmarks.

Remember that pad of paper (or digital list) you kept when you cleared your desk? Use it to capture what needs to get done.

Here's how it works:

The task you need to remember: I have to create the Facebook ad on Canva before the end of the day.

Your next step: Close the Canva tab and write: *Make Facebook ad on Canva.*

The task you need to remember: I have to test the email campaign on ConvertKit by noon.
Your next step: Close the ConvertKit tab and write: *Test CK email campaign.*

Lastly, if you want to try that recipe tonight, bookmark the page. Yes, it's that simple. Let's not make this harder than it needs to be. Use your list and use your bookmarks.

Don't apply discipline to avoid clicking on tabs, getting distracted by email or Facebook, or losing focus on invoices and analytics. That's the amateur show. You, my friend, are entering pro focus status, and pros do not rely on willpower.

Number Four: Silence the phone.
It's hard to imagine there was a time when our phones weren't an appendage. Yes, they are an amazing source of information and communication, but as far as a distraction, they are numero uno.

Our phones are the biggest contributor to our distractions. By the way, turning your phone on vibrate doesn't make you less likely to check your phone. Your phone might not ring out loud but with every little shake, you still divert your attention, do a quick looky-poo to make sure to check out the video your friend sent you of her grandma on stilts.

It's all the same. Vibration mode does not improve the situation.

So, what can you do it about it?

Remember how I suggested you turn off all your notifications? Chances are you didn't do it, and even more chances that you're not going to do it at all. So, I have a little trick for you, and it works like magic.

This one you can do. You will do. You must do.

It's easy-peasy and isn't nearly as scary as turning off all your notifications or your ringers. It has a massive impact on focus and getting the right things done. In fact, it requires you to turn something ON.

Hop on your smartphone, click on Settings, and swipe the Do Not Disturb button. That's it. Easy as pie. When Do Not Disturb is enabled, call and alerts will be silenced for real, *not the vibrating kind*, while still having access to your apps, photos, and everything on the interwebs.

In other words, with one little swipe of your finger, you truly squash the distractions, while in control of accessing information when you need it. If you can't promise yourself to take this one small action when you're trying to focus, well ...you're not that serious about trying to focus.

There is one more piece to this methodology to take it from a base hit to a home run. Let's jump into that in the next empowering strategy.

Number Five: Commit to a time period.

Since you are an ambitious go-getter, committed to getting massive results in your career and life, you have excitedly agreed to put the last four distraction-free strategies into action. Now imagine this:

It's 9:00 a.m. You've cleared your desk (except for that paper pad), you've turned off the notifications, you've closed the tabs, aaaaand you've put your phone on Do Not Disturb. Way to follow directions, by the way!

You are ready to focus all morning long. You're going to sit down and knock out that entire social media strategy you've been putting off for weeks. You are a badass focus machine!

Uh... how long do you think that's going to last? In other words, how long will that sacred focus of yours going to stay intact?

I wish I had a stat for you, like: 87% of people will not make it to twelve minutes, but I don't. I can only go by my personal experience and compare that with hundreds of clients. From that, I can tell you twelve minutes is a stretch. It's more along the line of 3-7 minutes.

Why? You've done all the things the productivity lady, *that's me*, told you. Why is it still so hard?

Because without a specific time period you're not working against a boundary. The idea of staying focused without a time commitment adds so much weight to your project or task. Without a boundary, you have no goal, other than to work on your task.

...but for how long? 30 minutes? One hour? Two hours? All day?!

Without knowing how long you're working for, all you can really think about is that you're losing time and that you have so much more to do. You can barely focus on the task at hand while warding off distracting thoughts of calls to make, emails to send, posts to update, people to answer, lessons to create and everything else on your ever-growing, overwhelming list.

To alleviate this fear, distraction, and anxiety, it's crucial to put a parameter around your focus time. Knowing you will focus for 20 minutes or 40 minutes or 7.83 minutes, instantly gives you a goal to strive for and a fixed amount of time to work against.

I've tried a dozen different ways to do this and by far the most effective, *...not to mention truly the easiest*, is to use Pomodoro's. If you've never heard of Pomodoro, you're in for a treat. If you have heard of it (but not using it) keep reading. Either way, it will Change. Your. Life.

The Pomodoro Technique is a time management method developed by Francesco Cirillo in the late 1980s. The main idea of the technique is to work in blocks of 25-minutes intervals (called Pomodoro sessions), followed by a 5-minute break. Your full attention should remain on one task during each Pomodoro session and each short break requires you to step away from your work to rest.

Focused, intentional, uninterrupted work sessions that by the way, require you to take regular breaks. Can it get any better?

"...and the result?", you may be asking?

Super improved productivity. Like, if you commit to using these 25 minutes of amazingness, all day there's a good chance you'll get more done than you have in a week.

Here's what the first couple hours might look like in your newly improved Pomodoro workday.

9:00 a.m. - 9:25 a.m. – *Pomodoro #1:* Create a repository of Facebook images

9:25 a.m. - 9:30 a.m. – *5-minute Break:* Check Facebook *Thank goodness! That 25 minutes without it was stressful!*

9:30 a.m. - 9:55 a.m. – *Pomodoro #2:* Schedule 3 months of posts using those images

9:55 a.m. - 10:00 a.m. – *5-minute Break:* Get your second cup of coffee

10:00 a.m. - 10:25 a.m. – *Pomodoro #3:* Respond to emails *Yes, your 25 minutes can and should be used for emails.*

10:25 a.m. - 10:30 a.m. – *5-minute Break:* Check Facebook again

...and so on...

Compare this to your current day.

9:00 a.m. - 10:22 a.m. – Get sucked into email ...*even though you told yourself you'd check it just for 10 minutes.*

10:22 a.m. - 10:47a.m. – Check Facebook

10:48 a.m. - 11:00 a.m. – Work on a to-do list for the day and get totally overwhelmed

See how much more you got done (in less time) in the first scenario using Pomodoros? *It's simply mahvelous, dahling.*

<u>Important Tip</u>: Use a Pomodoro app. Do not use your watch, laptop clock or wall clock to time yourself. How many times have you looked at your watch and then five minutes later have no idea what time it is? It's easy to lose track this way. Also, there is a psychological advantage about working against a timer. Search "Pomodoro" in your phone apps. I use FocusKeeper but there are a few options that all have the 25-minute timers.

Ok, you are doing awesome, and you are well on your way to being an undistracted and totally intentional "Focus Queen". It's not the quantity of time that really matters as much as the quality of what you do during this time. Hang in there, the final strategy is up.

Number Six: Let other people know.
You're getting so close to getting and staying focused. Let's say you do all the things. You sit down at 9am with a cleared desk, tabs closed, phone on Do Not Disturb, computer notifications off, set your Pomodoro, but yet, you're still feeling uneasy.

What if my clients are trying to get in touch with me? Will they think I'm ignoring them, or that I'm not doing my job well? What if they wither away in irrepressible sadness from not hearing from me sooner?!

We're so used to being accessible all the time... reacting, reacting, reacting.

Hear the text, respond right away.
Feel the phone, answer it immediately.
Get the email, type right back.

We've already established that we're putting a false sense of urgency towards these focus suckers, but how do you break the habit and reset expectations?

Let. People. Know.

Yup, just let people know what they can expect from the new focused you.

There are two super simple ways to do this.
#1: Change your email auto-responder
#2: Change your voicemail

Update your modes of communication to reflect your focus time. For example, you might change your voicemail to say:
"You've reached (insert name here). Sorry to have missed your call. I typically check my voicemail at noon and 4pm. Please leave me a message and I'll get back to you by the end of the day. If it's an emergency text me at 123-456-7890."

You might turn on your email autoresponder that goes something like this:
"I will be in a meeting until 11am. I will respond to your email by the end of day. If you need my attention urgently, please resend with URGENT in the title of the email. Thank you!"

Then, just like that, you've set your clients, friends, and Great Aunt Emma's expectations. By setting your communication modes accordingly you put people at ease by ensuring them you've received their message and will take care of them soon.

Voila! Expectations set for them and anxiety taken off of you.

So, there you have it, six simple ways to put the kibosh on never-ending distractions and get you into flow, so you can get more done than ever before and close out every day feeling awesome.

Before we wrap up this chapter, I want to leave you with this last message. If you think avoiding distractions is hard, in the grand perspective of life and your business, it isn't.

Cancer is hard.
Not having a roof over your head is hard.
Extracting a tooth without Novocaine is hard.

Closing tabs and tapping a button on a timer is simple.

You can read this over and over but until you take action, nothing is going to change.

Follow Mules (Mridu's Rules) And Action Steps To Feeling Less Distracted

Don't move on to the next Chapter before going through the next short exercise:

1. Clear your desk.
2. Close the tabs.
3. Turn off your computer notifications.
4. Set your phone to Do Not Disturb.
5. Use a Pomodoro timer!
6. Change your email and voicemail (only if you're still feeling uneasy after steps 1-5).
7. Breathe deep. Relax. Try these tips. Feel success. Have failure. Then get back on them again. Hour after hour, day after day.

You will start catching yourself getting distracted and will want to pull yourself out of it. Awareness is a great feeling. Don't beat yourself up over losing focus but celebrate the fact you are armed with the simple tools to overcome your interruptions and get back on track.

You can do this, fearless warrior. The quieting of your anxiety and the success of your business lies in your ability to make the simple things a habit.

Get back to the basics.
Regain your focus.
Feel confident that you will accomplish more of the right things.

(Come on over to
www.lifeisorganized.com/rightthings for a free
resource for all the exercises).

Chapter Two:
Make The Impossible Possible

(Code Letter: "C")

Heels. Makeup. Swanky top. Typical Thursday night in Manhattan. Hitting a bar or two or three... with my girlfriends. My friend, Sonia, invited me to join her at her friend's birthday party in Soho (NYC). The birthday guy and I had casually met a couple times earlier, but this night in May, the 15th to be exact, would change my life.

Several cocktails into the night, the guy and I hit it off. Like, real good. Post party we meandered to my favorite diner, where we talked over french fries and to my horror, I'm pretty sure I showed him my mashed potato mouth squirm routine. Clearly, a total turn on. Somehow, magically, ...*I'm sure it had nothing to do with the 8 drinks he had,* he kissed me.

After calling in sick the next day post my 5:00 a.m. escapade, we spent the entire day together, Sonia and I ended up hanging out in his apartment. His real grown-up pad with adult furniture, and I'm not talking Ikea, photo frames with actual family members *not the black and whites ones that come with the frame,* and what at first glance looked like a full set of matching dishes.

Add those pleasant surprises to what was turning out to be a smart and funny personality ...dare I say I was, cautiously optimistic about the possibilities. When he added the words, *I was definitely not expecting* "Want a Chips Ahoy?" I knew I was in trouble. I had no idea there were other 30+- year-old adults who proudly indulged in my favorite childhood cookies.

Fast-forward two inseparable months together, he literally swept me off my feet at the Cloisters on a beautiful Saturday morning. Overlooking the botanical gardens, he requested a photo from a passerby, sat me on a stone ledge as he bent on one knee and asked if I would make him the happiest guy in the world.

What. Was. Happening?!

Two days shy of our two-month anniversary, he was holding a gorgeous Tiffany cut stone and asking for my hand in marriage. I kept repeating the only three words any woman in this situation could muster up.

"Oh my God! Oh my God! Oh my God!"

I think that might have been followed up by an equally ridiculous and non-committal: "Are you serious?!"

Somewhere around the 8th "Oh my God" he asked: "Is that a yes?"

I'm not sure how I was able to belt out a "ya-huh" as I swear, I wasn't breathing, I threw my shaking arms around him and sniffled like a baby, and as they say, the rest is history.

Speaking of historical moments, as if the 58-day marathon dating session didn't keep even close friends and family hypothesizing how far we were into pregnancy, we had yet another shocker to add.

As we began the search for wedding venues, we quickly realized we were limited on spaces that could accommodate our wedding size in the city.

This is probably where I should insert a little something about our big, fat, Indian wedding. Since I was a girl, it was ingrained in me that I would have a huge wedding, and as I had attended countless other Indian weddings in my 20's, I knew the number was going to be about 500. Yes, 500 people.

Given that number and the fact that we wanted to get married in NYC and since we didn't want to wait forever, we narrowed our search. A space that we fell in love with was available the following spring or fall...*wait for it*...in October. About two and a half months away.

I thought my fiancé would freak out at this option, realize what he had done and run the other way, but instead, he was pumped about the October date. He told me that the biggest decision was deciding to get married. He didn't see any point of putting it off after that.

So we did it. We moved forward with the date. I remember telling my in-laws about our timeframe and my future mother in law saying there was no way we (as in a collective family "we") could pull it off in such a short time.

It wasn't *just* the wedding.

There was the engagement party, wedding shower, bachelor and bachelorette parties. There would be a pooja (prayer ceremony), a mendhi (henna party), a sangeet (like a dress rehearsal, with tons of dancing and singing), the chura (giving away ceremony) amongst nights of hosting family.

We Indians do not kid around.

Having serial dated for nearly a decade in the crazy world of Manhattan, I had waited long and hard for this moment. For this man. For this time in my life. There was nothing stopping me from marrying the love of my life and having the wedding of my dreams… and we were doing it in two months.

Together, with both families, we brainstormed, outsourced, collaborated, delegated, and compromised to pull it off.

Food, drinks, entertainment, linens, guest lists, chairs, tables, DJ's, bands, flowers, return gifts, speeches, hotels, centerpieces, themes, party favors, decorations, for the:

- Engagement party (150 guests)

- Pooja (100 guests)

- Mehndi (100 guests)

- Sangeet (400 guests)

- Chura (75 guests)

(plus, wedding shower and bachelor and bachelorette parties) AND the grand cougar of them all...

493 of our closest friends and family at the Puck Building in Soho on October 27th, celebrated our love and excitement to be with one another.

All planned in 10 weeks.

We made the impossible, possible.

Guess what? You can too.

When you are committed to your priorities, you can accomplish anything you want.

We all have times when we figure out a way to get what we want, even when we don't have time.

The day you had no time to deal with your overflowing papers but spent two hours finding the perfect outfit when you got that last-minute invite to drinks and dinner.

The weekend you had no time to work on the garage but managed to binge watch five episodes of Scandal.

The months you had no time for working out but kept up hourly relationships on Facebook, Instagram, or Snapchat.

Which brings me to the bigger question: What are your true priorities?

What are the most meaningful goals in your work and life?

At the end of this week, this month, this year, what is it that you want to accomplish? What would make you feel successful? What would make you really, truly, "I'm bursting with joy and pride", happy?

You might need to sit and think about this for a few minutes, or maybe even hours. Chances are you haven't thought about your true priorities in a long time. *How do you want to live your life?*

Your priorities are different than mine and different than your spouse or best friend. They are your own personal goals and they will change and evolve over time.

Here's the funny thing. Even if you can rattle off your true big priorities right this second, you're probably not making them the most important goals in your life. You're probably letting other distractions like email, TV, busy work, and other time wasters get in the way of what you know you really should be doing.

Here's a tool I use for myself and with my clients to help them determine where their time is going and more importantly, where they should be putting it instead.

Welcome to the Eisenhower Matrix: Your Tool For Getting The Right Things Done

You may have heard about or seen the Eisenhower Matrix. Eisenhower's strategy for taking action and organizing your tasks is simple. **Using the decision matrix below**, you separate your actions based on four possibilities.

1. Urgent and important (tasks you will do immediately)

2. Important, but not urgent (tasks you will schedule to do later)

3. Urgent, but not important (tasks you will delegate to someone else)

4. Neither urgent or important (tasks that you will eliminate)

The great thing about this matrix is that it can be used for broad plans ("How should I spend my time each week?") and for smaller, daily plans ("What should I do today?").

Here's how your matrix might be set up for your daily activity.

	Q1	Q2
	URGENT	**NOT URGENT**
IMPORTANT	**DO** Do it now. • Write today's blog	**DECIDE** Schedule a time to do it. • Exercise • Plan next quarter's strategy • Reach out to prospects • Call mom and dad
NOT IMPORTANT	**DELEGATE** Who can do it for you? How can I automate? • Pay bills (automate this) • Respond to certain emails • Book flights and hotels • Share resources • Schedule meetings	**DELETE** Eliminate it. • Social media time wasting • Watching TV • Perfecting website (again!)
	Q3	Q4

To get meaningful work done (and feel awesome at the end of each day), we should be navigating our day in order of the quadrants: 1, 2, 3 & 4. However, we typically spend most of our days going backward: 4, 3, 2, 1. Maybe you'll get that crisis out of the way (quadrant one) but get buried back in quadrants 3 & 4 right after that.

How often have you gotten sucked into email, social media, or phone calls, when your strategy, planning, family time, and exercise have taken a back seat? That is because we have lost sight between what is urgent and what is important.

> *"What is important is seldom urgent and what is urgent is seldom important."*
> *-Dwight Eisenhower*

I absolutely love this quote. We are urgency addicts and we give urgency to tasks that simply aren't. We react to emails, texts, and new stories as if they are emergencies. We allow them to throw us off course, divert our attention and impede our results.

Here's what is urgent:

- Your son/daughter calls from the side of the highway. Their car is broken down and they need help.

- Your mom is feeling pains in her chest and doesn't know what to do.

- Your client is on his way to a Board meeting where he is presenting your new marketing idea and he lost his flash drive and needs your summary asap.

- These are requests we should respond to with urgency.

Here's what's not urgent BUT we treat like they are:

- CNN news alert: NFL Players Reason for Skipping White House Visit

- Facebook update: Best weekend ever with my besties!

- Text message: Pumps or wedges? What goes best with this dress?

- Email notification: Can you do lunch on Thursday?

I know you see the difference between these requests, yet we react to them with equal urgency.

Meanwhile, the things that are super important in your life, *aren't* given that type of urgency. Like, exercise, being present with your family, financial planning, and business strategies.

What if we gave those priorities the same urgency that we do the article you had to share on "America's Best Spas"?

To sum it up: urgent tasks are things that you feel like you need to react to: emails, phone calls, texts, news stories. *Keep in mind tasks that feel urgent are usually part of other people's goals, **not yours.***

Meanwhile, in the words of Brett McKay, "Important tasks are things that contribute to our long-term mission, values, and goals." These tasks are usually part of your own personal goals.

When it comes to your business, your top priorities might be sales, marketing, networking, building relationships, creating systems, getting a promotion, writing a book, or developing a new product or service.

When it comes to the most meaningful personal goals, your top priorities might be getting your home organized, losing weight, implementing a consistent morning routine, being present, spending more time with your family, or learning how to knit.

What are your big priorities? What are your core professional goals? What are your core personal goals?

Take action now by printing and filling out the Eisenhower Matrix. You can find it here as a free resource at www.lifeisorganized.com/rightthings.

Once you've identified your top priorities both professionally and personally, ask yourself if you're setting yourself up for success to reach them. Are you focusing on what's most important to you, or are you constantly distracted by everything else on your overflowing plate?

Do you find that your priorities take the backseat to emails, social media, appointments, interruptions, phone calls, and going down the random rabbit hole?

If so, then maybe this scenario sounds familiar.

You come into work at 9 o'clock *or go upstairs to your office if you work at home like me.* You promise yourself you're going to sit and focus and get your most important things done for the day.

Hot cup of joe, cleared desk, situated in your comfy chair and then BOOM. You do it. You'll just take a quick lookity-poo at your email. No big deal. Just a scan. A short overview. A simple check and then back to business as planned.

Forty-three and a half minutes later you've successfully read reviews of the hottest restaurants in town, signed up for a webinar, downloaded Kroger coupons, and responded to your colleague about an event…that is happening six weeks from now. *Yes, quite the urgent matters.*

In a panic, you realize you only have ten minutes before you head to a meeting and that doesn't give you much time to focus on that strategy you really should be doing.

You may as well jump back into email and get some more urgent matters taken care of. *We really are quite good salespeople, as we've convinced ourselves that this is the "productive" thing to do). No big deal. You can focus on your big priorities later.*

You continue your day like this and now it's about 3 or 4 o'clock and guess who has no energy to be thinking about social media strategies, sales proposals, or hitting the gym? YOU.

Your brain is fried. Your body is tired. Your energy is used up, and your attitude is spent.

You've already done a good day's work *Remember how busy you were?!* so you'll just tackle those big priorities tomorrow. No big deal. Until tomorrow morning hits and guess what happens?

You come into work at 9 o'clock *or go upstairs to your office if you work at home like me.*

You promise yourself you're going to sit and focus and get your most important things done for the day.

Hot cup of Joe, cleared desk, situated in your comfy chair and then BOOM. You do it. You'll just take a quick lookity-poo at your email. No big deal. Just a scan. A brief overview. A simple check and then back to business as planned.

Until you look up and it's noon. Whhhaaaattt? How did that happen? …and the cycle starts again.

It's like the movie "Groundhog Day", except the glaring difference is you actually have control of changing your circumstances.

Chances are, you don't. By 4 o'clock you might finally be ready to jump into the "real work" but your brain and body have a different idea.

As you continue to procrastinate working on your big priorities, one of two very terrible scenarios play out.

Terrible scenario #1:
You've procrastinated so much that now you're under a deadline, so you've got to cram to get your work done, and that's rarely a good situation. You're under the gun which means you're working late, skipping the gym, eating crap, feeling cranky, snapping at your family, and not working at your optimal performance. No bueno.

Terrible scenario #2:
You don't get to your big priorities for months. Sometimes years. Ouch. Let's say your big priorities aren't deadline driven, like losing ten pounds or developing a new skill, like podcasting. No real deadline around it, so three months go by. Six months go by. One year goes by and guess what? Ten pounds still hanging around and no podcast on the horizon.

Both scenarios are sucky.

On the other hand, imagine you started off your day addressing and working on your big priorities. Fully focused, uninterrupted, full of energy - progressing on your big goals. No more getting distracted by InstaStories, sucked into email, or interrupted by texts. Simply focusing on the tasks that will truly move your life forward.

Imagine you intentionally started your day this way for a set period of time before taking care of any of your other "stuff" on your list... or in your inbox.

Imagine, first thing every day you meditated, made sales calls, wrote a Chapter in your book, strategize a quarter's worth of FB posts, went for a walk, had technology-free breakfast with your kids, outlined a marketing funnel, or systemized an invoicing process.

Could you imagine the possibilities as you continued to do that day after day after day? Can you picture the magnitude of progress you'd make in a week? A month? Three months?

You might be thinking, *"That sounds great...in a dream world, but let's talk reality. My phone is blowing up before I grab coffee, I have meetings first thing, I'm always drowning in a crisis, or there's no way I can't get on email first thing in the morning."*

In that case, let me introduce you to my productivity bestie. The be all, end all of getting the right stuff done. The master of consistently moving the needle in your personal and professional goals.

Your "Power Hour."

Your Power Hour may be the most critical hour of your business, career, relationship, and life.

Yes, it is that powerful.

Your Power Hour is the first hour of your day to focus on your big priorities.

I actually have, and recommend, two Power Hours each day. One for your personal priorities and one for your professional priorities. ...but we'll get into that in just a bit.

Here's how your Power Hour works.

Before you do anything else, like read and respond to emails, jump into social media, scroll your phone, deal with an "emergency," – Commit to your top priorities.

Hint: These are usually the tasks that constantly get pushed to the end of the day or inadvertently procrastinated. Those things *you know you really should be doing* but aren't. (Again, think exercising, sales calls, networking, strategy, building relationships, journaling, planning, and creating. All those tasks and goals you listed in Quadrant Two of the Matrix).

There are two keys to making sure your Power Hour actually happens:

Key #1: Put it on your calendar. Front and center. First thing every day. Perhaps it's blocked off on your calendar from 8:30 a.m. to 9:30 a.m. or 10:00 a.m. to 11:00 a.m. or 6:00 a.m. to 7:00 a.m. There's no hard and fast rule about what time, other than have it scheduled before you fall into the quicksand of your other work and get distracted. This will help reinforce this practice for you as well as let other people who have access to your schedule, know that you are busy.

If you have a meeting first thing that cannot be changed, schedule your Power Hour for the first hour when you return to your office.

Key #2: Use a timer. I recommend doing two Pomodoro's during your Power Hour.

Quick review on this. (You can also read about this again in Chapter One). Set your Pomodoro (or Focus Keeper) app for one 25-minute session. If you need the 5-minute break to stretch, pee, get coffee or scan your email, by all means, do it. As soon as you hear the "ding" move right into your second 25-minute

Pomodoro. That's it. That's your Power Hour for the day.

(If you're in flow and don't need that first 5-minute break, work through it and go 55 minutes straight. Then, be sure to take your second 5-minute break to refresh your brain and energy).

Do those two tasks and you'll increase your Power Hour success tenfold.

I have had clients that have transformed their entire business using The Power Hour.

Creating a cohesive and comprehensive training manual was a priority for one of my clients. Managing operations across eight unique retail spaces and managing 500 employees rarely left her five minutes to think about this, never mind the months she would need to make it happen.

However, when she implemented the Power Hour, her first hour of every day was solely focused on this document. That's all, nothing else.

That's five hours a week. Twenty hours a month. (Monday - Friday)

She completed the training manual in six weeks. *Six weeks!* She had been wanting to work on it for over two years.

Was it hard to not check email during that time or answer calls or texts? Sure, at first.

When she was a week into the process and saw she was already making significant progress with her manual, this priority went from sitting in the back seat, to traveling with a first-class ticket.

She realized that her business, stores, and people would not fall apart if they had to wait an extra 30 minutes to speak with her or get her attention.

She recognized that getting up 45 minutes earlier to get ahead on her morning would not kill her – or even partially maim her.

She remembered what it felt like to contribute in a meaningful way and how much joy she felt in reaching her goals.

Think about the progress YOU could make in any goal, task, or project if you put in 20 solid, focused hours a month.

Motivation comes from action. When you take daily action that leaves you feeling accomplished, valuable, and like you've added to the growth and results of yourself, your team,, and your family, you will be less resistant to "the work."

When you see and feel your success, your inner motivation will kick into overdrive, which is far more fun and exciting than having to push it out of you.

Caveat: For the majority of people, the morning is the best time for their heavy thinking work. They perform at their highest levels after a good night's sleep and a good morning routine.

However, there's a small percent of people that work best at other times during the day. I've worked with clients that knew they were most effective between 5:00 p.m. - 7:00 p.m. or even from 9:00 p.m. - 11:00 p.m. IF this is you, then adjust your Power Hour accordingly. Personally, I'm fried by the end of the day or evening, so my best work is in the morning.

I mentioned earlier that I recommend a personal Power Hour and a professional Power Hour.

You have personal goals that are just as important, if not more crucial, than your professional goals. You know that exercise, eating well, meditation or prayer, journaling and quiet time will help you energize your body and brain and start your day from a place of calm and positive energy. Create a personal Power Hour to achieve these goals.

To make my Power Hour(s) effective, I've committed to getting out of bed one hour earlier than I used to. That is not easy for someone who's never considered herself a morning person. One hour used to feel like a huge sacrifice. Until I started seeing and feeling the results.

Through a huge relief of stress, I'm committed to a morning meditation and exercise, and a massive improvement in my business results, I've nearly quadrupled my income by focusing on revenue-generating activities before anything else, getting up an hour earlier isn't the worst thing in the world anymore.

If you know that tweaking your morning routine will impact your day and results, I highly recommend reading "The Miracle Morning" by Hal Elrod. Add that to your book list, after you finish reading this one of course.

If you haven't set aside time in the morning for yourself in the past, one hour might feel too challenging. So, start with 25-30 minutes. Take a 15-minute walk or do a 10-minute stretch. Enjoy your coffee in peace. Read positive affirmations for 5 minutes. *Again, read "The Miracle Morning".*

I already know that you will fall into one of two camps after reading all about this deep work, focused strategy time and/or personal care time:

1. You're really excited about giving your Power Hour (or two) a shot. You know it requires commitment, but the idea of moving the needle in goals every single day pumps you up and is exactly what you need to be doing.

2. You like this idea in theory but have already thought about half a dozen reasons why you can't make it happen, like, "I have to get my kids to school", or "I'm always stuck in traffic." "My clients will die if I don't give them attention every minute of the day."

If you fall in camp two, here's the deal. Yes, you have a busy life. Yes, you have a lot on your plate, *I'm pretty sure that's why you're reading this book,* but if you don't change the way you're doing things, nothing will change. You will continue to wake up feeling overwhelmed, scattered throughout the day, and hanging low on success every evening.

The truth is, if you're serious about lowering stress, taking control of your time and life, and having more success than ever before, you will figure out a way to make your Power Hour happen.

Here are some ideas.

- o Wake up one hour earlier.

- o Make lunches, pick out your outfit, print directions, get bags packed at night.

  - o Do all those little tasks that you leave for the morning done at night, so you not only get through your morning feeling calm, you easily find time to get your high priority stuff done.

- o Let your clients know you have a standing morning meeting from 9:00 a.m. - 10:00 a.m. so you are happy to meet with them at 10 o'clock or later.

- o Let other people on your team know that unless the office is on fire you are not to be interrupted until 10:00 a.m. (Or start your day at 8:00 a.m. and you can take calls and questions after 9:00 a.m.)

- o If you have a door (or work in a cubicle) put up a sign that says: *Deep work until 10:00 a.m. Please do not disturb.*

- o Change your email autoresponder to say you check your emails at 11:00 a.m. or you're in a morning meeting. That way you've set expectations for anyone trying to contact you while alleviating stress on yourself.

I've created Power Hours in companies with over a hundred people. I've created Power Hours with departments of fifteen. You can do it with your team or group too. Get everyone on the same page about focusing on their most important work first thing.

Implement a policy that no one will send interoffice emails or set up meetings during this first hour of the day. Everyone will benefit from this time. Everyone will make progress. You, your team, and your organization will start their day feeling accomplished and getting better results, faster. It is the ultimate win-win.

When everything feels overwhelming

After a day of back to back meetings and appointments you come back to your office with a pit in your stomach. 126 emails, 13 missed calls, and too many texts to count. You feel like you're drowning in quicksand, head first. You look at your to-do list, more like pages of lists, and everything seems important.

It's overwhelming not to mention, paralyzing.

How do you stay focused on those priorities (quadrant 1 & 2) again? How do you even remember what are in those quadrants?

I've tried tons of list making tools, spreadsheets, apps, and planners to help me prioritize, but there's one strategy that hands down works the best.

Before I reveal this nifty time and sanity-saving tool, I've got to tell you, it's pretty technical. So, if you're not as technology savvy as I am, don't fret. With some trial and error, I promise you can catch on to this.

Are you ready for the big reveal?

The secret strategy of top productivity experts?

The life-changing tool that only super organized people know about?

Wait for it…Wait for it…

It. Is. A…

Sticky Note! (Fooled you, didn't I?)

Yup, a sticky note. It's my secret weapon and without one I'm not nearly as effective or focused as I know I can be.

So, here's how this highly technical strategy works.

Every morning I write down my "Top Three". My "Top Three" are the three things I must get done that day.

I also refer to my "Top Three" as my "Gotta Do" list. Not, I *should* do; not, I *might* do; not I *wanna* do, or I *could* do but – but the I *Gotta* Do. **No. Matter. What.**

These tasks are ones you currently don't do. For example, I wouldn't add "meditate" to my Top Three since this is already a part of my daily routine.

On the other hand, I would add:

- Write blog post

- Walk for 45 minutes

- Create and send the speaking contract

No matter what, before my head hits the pillow, those three tasks must be completed.

The beauty of the sticky note is that it is visual. It helps you focus and have clarity throughout the day. I usually stick it on my laptop screen so when I get back from meetings and appointments, I have a visual anchor to keep me on task.

Plus, it's portable. I can grab my note and stick it to my notebook on my way to an appointment.

Narrowing my top tasks down to three can be tricky some days when it feels like I have a hundred things to get done. So, I ask myself: ***What three things would I have to complete to make me feel successful and happy today?***

Want to know a secret to staying motivated and inspired?

Completing what you set out to do.

Too many days we have all these goals we want to achieve but then we get distracted, don't complete them, and feel like failures. Which totally sucks because over time this has an impact on our self-esteem and our confidence about what we can achieve.

With the Top Three priorities planned and crossed off, you end each day feeling like a winner, and that my sweet friend, motivates you to keep at it the next day and the day after that and the day after that.

Seem too easy?

Sometimes the most powerful and effective tools are. Don't let the simplicity fool you or leave you thinking "really?" before you even start.

Yes, you will still have a lot of emails and calls to get through after completing those three, but you know you won't end the day without making progress on your most important priorities. That is the only way you will feel happy and accomplished.

Have faith in yourself that you will figure out a way to get the other stuff done.

In fact, when you have less time to deal with your email, you will respond more efficiently, delete more diligently, and naturally select what is truly important.

When you have little time, you'll be amazed how many less hours you'll spend reading random articles, going down the social media rabbit hole, or watching laughing baby videos.

I unexpectedly lost power at my house recently. No internet, phone, heat, light...I didn't know what to do with myself. By the time I got to speak to a real live human at the electric company Thank goodness my cell phone still worked. I was 90 minutes into total hysteria.

Meanwhile, I got a call that my son wasn't feeling well, and I needed to pick up him. After scooping him up from school, buying medicine, playing caretaker at home, and still wrangling with Donna at the electric company, I'd lost the entire day. It was nearly 3:00 p.m. before the interwebs and lights were back on.

I was sure the world must have fallen apart while I was on my one-day sabbatical. Everyone must be trying to get in touch with me. Who could survive my disappearance?!

Apparently, everyone.

All was fine. My clients were still alive and well, and business was, well, business. I caught up on all the "important" stuff in about two focused hours.

It reminded me of how much nonsense and false sense of urgency I create for myself, for no good reason.

Feeling accomplished at the end of each day is more important than how many to-do's you get to cross off.

It's about taking action on the stuff that matters most.

Here's what matters most right now.

Get crystal clear on your big priorities and commit to making progress on them every day.

Follow Mules (Mridu's Rules) For Feeling Awesome
Don't move on to the next Chapter before going through the next short exercise:

1. Take 5-10 minutes right now to time block tomorrow.

2. Add a 10-minute block at the end of each day to plan for the next.

3. Print and fill out the Eisenhower Matrix. (if you were serious about this, yours is already done) Go to: www.lifeisorganized.com/rightthings

4. Commit to your Power Hour(s). Like, for real. This is a commitment to YOU.

5. What actions will you put in place to ensure it happens?

    a. (Ex: get it on your calendar, wake up earlier, no email before 10:00 a.m., and change your voicemail).

As your personal Accountability Coach, let me know you took action. Email me right here:

mridu@lifeisorganized.com. I read and respond to every message, and I cannot wait to hear about your success. Here's to getting more of the right things done and feeling accomplished!

Chapter Three:
Sick of Getting Steamrolled?

(Code Letter: "T")

I've always loved Halloween. Indulging into the life of someone entirely different than yourself, even for a few short hours, has always intrigued me. Combining that with a chance to harness my creativity had me thinking about my getup throughout the year. Buying a costume seemed so effortless and unchallenging. I wanted to sew, paint, and construct my costume even if it, or pieces of it, were available at Party City. I took pride in my ingenuity and couldn't wait for the world to see my creation every year.

I should also let you know that I was not out to look pretty. I spent the other 364 days of the year blow drying my hair, applying makeup, and matching my outfits. Why would I want to do the same on this creative day? To my mother's demise, I was never the cute cheerleader with pom-poms and ponytails or an adorable cat in a shapely black leotard and furry ears.

One year, when my college roommate, Monica, and I were visiting my parents, we attended a costume party. Monica came out of my room in an adorable genie outfit: a camisole top, shrug with sheer sleeves spangled with sequin accents, a fringe of gold coins, and a matching veil.

I busted out attempting a less than average moonwalk, hand in crotch, jerry curled hair, glittering silver glove, and bolero red jacket with padded shoulders ...*which I'm proud to say, I sewed in myself.*

In my mother's best attempt to deflect her disappointment and redirect my energy she said: "Hey, I have an idea! Mridu, why don't you become a genie too!" I gave her an eye roll, followed by a "Really, mom?", grabbed my crotch again and unsteadily moonwalked through the kitchen. I'm pretty sure I hit the side of my head on the doorway before I made it out.

Fast-forward six years, I was living in Manhattan in my 400 square foot studio apartment. My brother and sister in-law lived eight floors above me, and we were throwing an awesome Halloween party between our two homes. It's amazing how many twenty-somethings you can fill in 400 and 800 square feet when alcohol and food are flowing on one of the best holidays of the year. *Yes, I know Halloween is not actually a holiday, but it really should be.*

I was pumped. I had worked long and hard on my costume and I couldn't wait for the "oohs" and "ahhs" over it.

"You made that yourself?"
"That's incredible!"
"Pure genius."

These days you can easily buy this costume, but two decades ago, before Amazon and "the' Google, it wasn't available in many stores and certainly not to the level of detail I had put into it. After deliberating political and social icons, historical figures and mystical characters, I landed on an interesting item in the food group category. Yes, many months in the making I resurrected: The Hot Dog.

Not just any hot dog, though. My hot dog was a 6-foot replica that draped over my head, oozing with ketchup, mustard, and relish. It even had a secret potty door so I could freely pee throughout the night. It. Was. A. Masterpiece.

I can't remember exactly how many weeks I put into the design and creation of my costume, but I do remember scheduling my days and hours around making it.

"Want to meet for drinks?"
"Um, not tonight. I'm perusing fabrics at The Salvation Army that would make for a good piece of mystery meat."

"Want to go shopping on Saturday?"
"Only if it involves buying cotton in bulk." (I really underestimated the amount I'd need to fill up that dog).

I blocked time around my work, gym routine, and social events that I'd already committed to. Back then I used my lavender paisley spiral bound paper planner (I'm a digital gal now) to mark in time between step aerobics and laundry to hand sew the tail flap or cut red felt in spiral-like waves for ketchup.

I'd schedule evenings when I didn't have to work late or celebrating a friend's birthday to sew in the suspenders on the inside of the dog to keep it up without straining my shoulders.

The big day arrived, and I was the by far the best damn hot dog you'd ever seen. In fact, the only hot dog in sight. I proudly put on my brown long sleeve shirt to match my almost six feet of cotton filled fabric, adjusted my straps, admired my perfectly placed relish, and tried out my pee door. I was set.

Then we decided to do shots.

Apparently, several of them before anyone arrived. I'm pretty sure I didn't eat much, as I spent most of the day piling furniture onto my bed, shoving photo frames, papers, and side tables into my closets to open up every square inch of space. I spent the rest of my time making appetizers and carefully laying out cheese and cracker platters because it would be ridiculous for a giant hot dog to serve anything less than classy.

Those shots hit me real hard. The last thing I remember is saying hi to my friend Nim, the shooting star, and then making a beeline for the toilet. In all my practice with the hot dog, walking in it, peeing in it, using my peripheral vision to talk to people on either side of me, not once did I think of how I would: a) quickly get it off in case of emergency or b) vomit without ruining it

Needless to say, I ended up with far more condiments on my hot dog than mustard and ketchup. My breakfast, lunch, and dinner the night before was all over that dog and no matter how hard I scrubbed, I smelled like hot dog vomit. One of my last memories before passing out, with 40 of my closest friends around me, was my sister in-law pulling it off of me, opening the garbage chute in the hallway, and watching weeks of hard work, not to mention my Halloween integrity, go down the metaphorical toilet. *It. Was. Bad.*

By now you might be wondering what is the moral of this incredible suspense thriller?

Never drink on an empty stomach?
It's a dog-eat-dog world out there?
Don't fool yourself into believing that Halloween is a real holiday?

It's this.

If it's not on your calendar, it doesn't happen.

In this dramatic sequence of my life, if I hadn't blocked out the time to design my outfit, research options, get to the stores, sew the pieces together; I would have been pulling an all-nighter just before the soiree. That would have made for one very cranky feeling hot dog, which is never a good way to show up as a hostess.

Protect your time like a mama bear protects her cubs. Use your calendar as the shield with which you protect your life and everything that is important in it.

Here's the cold hard truth. **If you don't protect your time, no one else will.**

...I don't have time to not be protecting my time.

There will always be emails to read, articles to peruse, emergencies to take care of, invites to attend to, as well as cries for help, requests for assistance, demands for support, and The Bachelor three-hour finale, vying for your attention. If you don't have time blocked, coveted, secured, and protected, something or someone else will take control of it.

How does time-blocking work? It's quite simple actually.

Step 1: Look at your to-do list and decide what your priorities are for the day. If this first step is stumping you, don't overthink it. Ask yourself: at 5:00 p.m. today, what will I have done over the last several hours to make me feel accomplished?

Hint: Your most important priorities are either deadline related or help you make progress towards a goal, like losing weight, making a sale or marketing yourself). Another hint: Go back to Chapter 2 all about priorities.

If you're still stumped, put a stake in the ground and pick 3-5 priorities. Just like that. For now, it is the exercise of blocking your time that is important.

So, you've picked: get to the gym, finish proposal for Wyatt Co., and pick up allergy medicine.

Great. Sounds like a pretty successful day. You've hit a personal goal, completed a proposal, and crossed off an important errand.

Step 2: Look at your calendar and everything you already have scheduled for the day. Usually, that consists of meetings, events, doctor's appointments, and social commitments. All the other white space? That's what you fill in with your top priorities. For example:

- Block out 7:00 a.m. - 8:00 a.m. for your workout
- Block out 10:30 a.m. - 11:30 a.m. to "Finish proposal for Wyatt Co."
- Block out 4:15 p.m. - 4:45 p.m. for the medicine pick up, on your way home from picking up the kids

Essentially, you are scheduling meetings with yourself to get your priorities done.

Here's why this is so important. Without self-meetings, there is little self-integrity. There is also a lot of time and energy wasted on confusion and constant reaction.

Think about your day as it currently is, with *only* meetings and appointments on your calendar. What happens to the rest of your time?

Does it get sucked up by emails? Unnecessary phone calls? Paralyzed by fear or confusion? Do you find yourself spinning your wheels for hours on end simply trying to figure out what to do next?

How often are you reacting, responding, and replying to everyone else's needs, emails, and requests? Are you distracted by social media, Google searches,and binging on Netflix? Do you get completely lost in re-organizing your desk, simply procrastinating what you know you should be doing?

These are typical signs of the ambitious person who's working from a lack of planning and an absence of methodology. Working this way, whether at home or an office environment, leaves you feeling unaccomplished, unsatisfied, and unworthy. You are far too valuable and brilliant to be living a life that makes you feel less than adequate.

Time blocking provides structure to your day, meaning to your hours, and impact on your priorities.

You'll spend less time thinking about "Should I work on my logo, or should I spend time on my sales script?" "Should I run my errands now, or should I work on my financials?" All that wasted thinking time, in which you spend hours spinning in circles, easily goes away. You've already invested the time to think that through, which means you get to simply look at your schedule and get cracking on your next to-do.

Truth be told, there are times when I love being told what to do, which is exactly what your time blocked schedule will do for you. It will hold you accountable, give you direction on what to focus on next and alleviate the pain and effort in figuring out your entire day every few minutes. It is truly a strategy that has transformed my life, my energy, and my results.

I often find I spend many sessions working on time blocking with my clients, because like with any new habit, it doesn't happen overnight. (And least not effectively). Here's the most common challenge they face and how to get over it.

Big challenge: These self-meetings are awesome in theory but here's the problem when you're the only attendee. If you don't feel like showing up, no one will know or even care for that matter, except you. Which makes it really easy to blow off or like us sneaky ones like to do, pretend it wasn't there in the first place.

Can you relate?

Maybe you've had a day just recently that went something like this...

You need to take care of a task you've been procrastinating for ages, so you do the right thing. You block time on your calendar to get it done. You've scheduled it for 2:00 p.m. 2:00 p.m. comes around, you completely ignore your reminder, and you move it to the next day. Tomorrow, 2:00 p.m. comes around and no surprise, you go through the same exercise and move it to the next day, and it goes on and on and on.

Why do we keep blowing off our scheduled tasks and then wonder why we never get to them?!
More importantly — how do we stop ignoring them?

There are a few factors to think about before you schedule another self-appointment that you are likely to blow off.

#1: Is your task realistic?

- Given your schedule, is it realistic that you get showered, dressed, lunches ready and kids out the door with a workout starting at 7:00 a.m.? Perhaps you need to push up your schedule to 6:00 a.m. which means getting out of bed by 5:30 a.m.

- Is it realistic to work out seven days a week? Maybe you need to schedule Monday, Wednesday and Friday workouts...with a trainer, you are paying real money to, so you actually commit to it.
- Is it realistic that you will make it all the way across town for an 11:00 a.m. meeting when your last appointment ends at 10:30 a.m.?

Don't schedule tasks without thinking through the time it will take for you to complete it as well as what else is going on in your world.

#2: Is your task too big? *This is usually the culprit!*

- Does "Write book" scare the bajesus out of you? No doubt you're gonna glaze over that reminder.
- Does "Get new job" make your heart sink, not to mention click "close" when that shows up on your schedule?
- Does "do tax reports" make you want to stick a fork in your eye? *...and totally ignore your calendar?*

The cure to this self-induced pain is to chunk down your big task into small tasks and schedule just ONE of them on your calendar instead.

For example, "Create outline for Chapter One" is way less overwhelming than "Write book."

"Put receipts in chronological order" is way less anxiety-inducing than "Do taxes."

Block time for a specific **small** task and see how much more inspired you feel to take action.

#3: Does it work with your energy level?

- Does it make sense to schedule your financial updates on Fridays at 4:00 p.m. when you are mentally and emotionally spent?
- Does working on a high brain activity, say analyzing results, make the most sense right after a heavy lunch?
- Is client strategy work more conducive first thing in the morning when your creativity is highest or at the end of the day when you're low on steam?

As a rule of thumb, I try to schedule high brain activities, (like strategy, writing, and planning), in the morning and process or admin work, (like papers, emails, and texts), in the afternoon. For most people, best work is done in the morning after a good night's sleep, exercise, and breakfast.

However, IF you are truly a night person (like about 10% of you out there), plan your high thinking time and work accordingly. The important thing is to be aware of your energy levels and work with, not against, them.

#4: Beware of recurring tasks.

As much as I love the efficiency of scheduling recurring tasks, they also make for the easiest ones to blow off. When I was trying to get into a habit of staying current on news, I took a dose of my own medicine and scheduled "Read news" at 4:00 p.m., from now until eternity. I bet you can guess how long that lasted. About three days. Then it was just another annoying reminder that I was shooing off my screen every day at 3:50 p.m. It simply reminded me of what I wasn't doing, slowly chipping away at my self-esteem.

Finally, I took it off but added it on my list of daily activities. When I was planning my day, (time blocking), I added "check news" every day, at a different time that made sense. Some days it was in the morning before I started my day, some days at night before I went to bed, and some days at 4:00 p.m. like I originally scheduled, over a cup of tea.

This idea of planning each day actually brings me to my next tip about uh, Planning. Each. Day.

I highly recommend making a ritual every Sunday evening to plan your week. By ritual, I mean make it relaxing and fun, not something you will dread. Pour a glass of wine, put on your favorite yoga pants, tell Alexa to play your favorite playlist, and grab your calendar or schedule. *By the way, this luxurious 15-20 minutes should be blocked on your calendar each week!*

Think about everything you have going on. Various projects, deadlines, travel, meetings, and events. Start with the low hanging fruit like any social commitments or appointments you may have that you haven't already put on your schedule. Next, think through deadline related projects and tasks.

Here's where the magic happens. Don't simply put "Send proposal to SBA" on Thursday at 5:00 p.m. Add in the time you need to work on it on Tuesday and Wednesday to get it done.

Block off 9:00 a.m. - 10:30 a.m. Tuesday to write your proposal.
Block off Wednesday 11:00 a.m. - 12:00 p.m. to strategize the costs for each phase.
Block off Thursday morning from 8:30 a.m. - 9:30 a.m. to proofread, finalize, and print it out.

Your success lies in your planning. Planning is not simply due dates but the time it takes to get the work done.

With a time blocked schedule, you get to make informed decisions about what to say yes to and what to say no to.

You get to make educated commitments about where to put your energy and where not to put your energy.

You get to be in charge of your time and day instead of other people or things (email, texts, calls) taking control of your time.

It goes a little something like this.

"Mridu, do you have a few minutes to read over my article to make sure it sounds okay?"

Me **Before** Time Blocking: *Sure, I'll just drop everything and act on your request immediately. This will distract me from my work, get me off schedule and blow how good I feel about getting done what I set out to do, but, Yes, give me your article...Right now!*

Me **After** Time Blocking: *I'd love to read your article. I bet it's awesome. I'm working on a proposal for a client and right after that, I've got to finish my blog. I have an opening from 10:45 - 11:00. Okay if I read it then?*

When your schedule is empty and requests come your way you have nowhere to turn but your helpful personality. So, you react, you help, you do, and you drop everything.

You have no evidence, no support, no basis from which to make a decision. Which means you're constantly operating from a place of distraction spiraling into a lack of focus, ultimately leaving you scattered, exhausted and confused about how your day got away from you without getting to the things that matter most.

On the other very much in control hand, by simply looking at your schedule you can move from a constant reactive state to a proactive one. Guess who's in the driver's seat then? Beautiful and empowered YOU!

Blocking your time will also take the paralysis out of your day. How much time do you spend procrastinating, thinking about what you should be working on next?

As the day goes on, your energy depletes and you're more likely to fall into the email blackhole or organize your file folders, to avoid what you really should be doing.

When you look at your calendar and see exactly what's coming up next, you alleviate the need to think about it over and over again.

Super Important Success Tip #1:
Take 5-10 minutes every evening to plan your next day.

It really is that simple (and fast) to start taking control of your life.

Look at the events and meetings on your schedule and then fill in that white space with exactly what you're going to do in that in-between time. The time it takes to do the work, the time it takes to travel, the time it takes to plan, the time it *all* takes.

If it's not on your calendar, it's *all* on your calendar. All the interruptions, the quickie questions, the urgent emails, the distracting texts, the unexpected calls, and the so-called emergencies.

This is one of those simple strategies that are not always easy to do, but I promise you, investing the few minutes at the end of each day to plan your tomorrow is a game changer. It's no guarantee that things will go your way, but why wouldn't you put yourself in the best position possible?

Super Important Success Tip #2:
Block your reactive work

Ok, so you've done the hard part. You've thought through your priorities and blocked your schedule, but keep in mind that as you block small periods of time for each task on your project list, you must focus on that and that alone. Do not work on five different tasks at the same time. *Go back to the first Chapter in this book if you need a refresher on avoiding distractions.*

Working on several tasks simultaneously may make you feel like you are moving forward on everything, but it is in fact, slowing down your productivity, wasting time and keeping you in a constant state of confusion and overwhelm.

In order to keep yourself focused, you have to make the time and space for your distractions too. Say whaaaat? Yes, in fact, distractions motivate your ability to stay focused. To concentrate, and to get into the flow of what you're doing.

Assign blocks of time for reactive work or you will spend your entire day in reactionary mode (emails, texts, Facebook, LinkedIn, phone calls etc). If a lot of your work is reactive, it will be natural to think this won't work for you, but that is a big fat lie you've come to believe. So, here's how you *can* make this work.

Step #1:
Make a list of all the things you get distracted by, that take your attention away from what you know you should be doing. In other words, time wasters. Let me help you get this started with my own list.

- Facebook
- Articles
- Blogs
- Pinterest
- Amazon
- LinkedIn
- House Projects
- News Alerts

Step #2:
Schedule 5-15 minutes for ONE of these types of distractions AFTER you've scheduled and completed 25-50 minutes of a non-time-wasting task. In other words, after you've worked on a priority for a focused period of time.

Step #3:
SET A TIMER. I think I need to repeat this one. SET A TIMER.
Set a timer for your allocated distraction time. (5, 10 or 15 minutes). If you don't set a timer, you know what happens. Your well-intentioned ten minutes turns into one hour and then you wonder where the time went and why you haven't gotten anything done! *Trust me, I have mastered this skill.*

Scheduling and budgeting time for your favorite distractions will help you avoid wasting time on it now. Using Facebook as a reward for getting through 50 minutes of work, will help you stay motivated and on task. Here are some examples:

- Schedule 30 minutes every 2 hours to respond to emails
- Schedule 45 minutes in the morning and at the end of the day to answer phone calls
- Schedule 15 minutes 3 times a day to answer texts

Without boundaries around our distractions, or worse, not creating dedicated time for them at all, they interrupt our thoughts and progress, moment-by-moment. The constant disruptions significantly lower productivity as our mind jumps back and forth between multiple tasks.

Additionally, social media, online shopping and browsing can be addicting and an easy saboteur of time. They keep us away from the things we really should be doing — for really long periods of time. I don't know about you, but the last time I tried to rely on willpower to stop my online addiction, I spent more time on my time waster than on my main work.

Thus, I'll say it again. Schedule your distractions and USE A TIMER!

This allows your other blocks of time to be far less interrupted, enabling you to get your best work done.

BIG, FAT HINT: This is where your Pomodoro's come in really handy.

Speaking of which, puh-lease do not take your self-care time for granted or assume it will just happen because it's a priority for you, and you have it all stored in your head.

It's just as important to block time for yourself and your personal goals as it is for team meetings and work goals. Block this time or it won't happen. Just like your dentist appointment or hair appointment, your personal goals and your health goals must be on your schedule. Every. Single. Day.

Prioritize the things that are important to you. Block time to work out, make meals, exercise, meditate, pray, grocery shop, run errands, read a book, and do nothing. Yes, do nothing. Me time. Creative time. Veg-out time. The Walking Dead binge-watching time. Create boundaries around your time to make sure that these things get your attention.

A common time block I have on my schedule is "catch up with hubby" time where we talk about things that have to do with our family or home.

Where should we plan our next vacation?
Do you have everything for the taxes?
Can I throw out this mail?
Can you pick up the kids at three o'clock on Thursday?
Why has our teenage son been possessed by the devil?

Simply seeing time blocked on the calendar keeps me on track and motivates me to have that conversation.

One last note on what to think about when you're time blocking. Don't forget to add in time for travel, setup, traffic, parking, and regrouping. Every time I make an appointment I add in "drive time" on both ends of the meeting with a buffer.

If I don't, and I get a meeting request, I'll simply look at my calendar and say "yes", because my calendar is free at 11:00 a.m. and then later realize I didn't take into account the driving time from my earlier meeting, 11:00 - 11:30, and look like a big doofus when I have to change the meeting time. Which is especially embarrassing as a "Productivity Expert."

Important self esteem note:
Time blocking requires time estimation - WHICH TAKES PRACTICE. Not estimating time to complete your work is one of the costliest mistakes I see ambitious people make. A to-do list is great but only half as valuable as a to-do list with time estimates.

Don't try to squeeze too much into one day. It's easy to underestimate how long a task will take. If you've never legitimately tracked your time before, this will take practice. Over time you WILL become a better time estimator. As you learn more about how you work, and how long each task really takes, your time block estimations will become more accurate, helping you become more productive.

If you don't know (or estimate) how long a task will take, you will always underestimate or overestimate and will struggle with planning. Be generous when you're calculating how long it will take you to finish a project. Make your best guess and then multiply the total by 1.2 to add a 20% cushion. Most tasks take longer than you think it will. Be realistic but mostly, be patient. You will get better at estimating your time the more you make it a practice.

NOTE: Time blocking does not equate to a lack of choice or creativity

One thing I hear all the time from my creative friends, or let's face it, anyone who is resistant to trying things a different way, is that they're worried time blocking will limit their creativity, spontaneity or choice. It is mechanical, rigid and waaaay too structured for their free-spirited, lifestyle.

I mean you left that 9 to 5 corporate job, working for the man, so you could set up your life the way you want to. Work in your pajamas, be at all the school events, and grow an amazing, profitable business while making an impact all on your terms. No pressure from other people, micromanaging bosses or company policies to adhere to.

So, if that's you...how's that working out for ya? Are you feeling less overwhelmed? More clear? Is your day running like a well-oiled machine?

I'm guessing if you've read this far, you're like the rest of us, just barely staying afloat. Mind racing with thoughts, ideas, and plans. Brain overloaded with next steps, follow-ups, and I should be's. Plate overflowing with to-do's, demands, and requests, and on top of it, wasting precious minutes and hours working from reactive mode, not getting to the things you know you really should be doing.

Blocking your time does not mean you'll have a lack of choice or that you'll be so steeped in rigidity that you can't get your creative juices running. It, in fact, gives you more freedom in your time, day, and brain.

Since you're not multi-tasking or wasting time on processing what to do next or getting caught up in constant reaction, you can spend your time effectively. Here's the clincher.

You can even block your creative time. It's true. Instead of trying to squeeze in bits and pieces here and there between answering calls, replying to texts, and glancing over emails, you can block thirty minutes, an hour, two hours, a half a day, for focused, uninterrupted brilliance.

You can only do this because you can see that you have three other periods of blocked time to respond to emails, and an hour to write your proposal, and forty-five minutes to go for a walk in the morning.

Blocking your whole day gives you the comfort and peace of mind that you've got the big things covered, so you can focus on one task at a time. For my writers, coaches, and artists, your focused creative time (also known as whitespace) is the lifeblood of your innovation.

As leaders, we need the time and space to digest information, analyze, and strategize what we need to do to reach our goals. Your results will multiply when you allow yourself the gift of working from a proactive vs. reactive mindset.

Which will leave you feeling much more accomplished, satisfied and simply happy at the end of each day.

You'll never know until you try.

Try blocking your time. All the way. Not just a couple of appointments and self-meetings here and there, but an entire day. From the time you wake up to when you go to bed.

Include a morning routine, self-care, driving to work, small chunks of what you'll work on during the day, email time, social media time, strategy time, creative time, walk time, lunch time, gossip time, more email time, Facebook time, I'm out of brain cells so I'll do easy work time, driving time, errand time, making dinner time, clean up time, mindless tv time, planning the next day time, reading time, and gratitude time. Will your day go exactly as planned? Probably not. However, if you're into releasing a giant weight from your shoulders every morning by having a plan in place, a roadmap to guide you through your day, a built-in accountability tool, a way to dodge reactive work and instead feel in control - Try. It. Out.

If accomplishing your priorities and making a significant impact on your goals faster is the kind of thing that lights you up, don't just read this. Do it. Sometimes you have to tune out your old habits to dial up new results.

Our productivity and motivation stem from how we feel during, and at the end of each day. If we don't have anything we're shooting for, we just tend to go through the motions and react to everything as it's thrown at us.

With time blocking you set goals for what you want to accomplish, and you set daily and hourly deadlines for those. I've found that when I do that, when I'm excited about what I'm working toward and have those goals that I'm trying to reach, I feel a lot more motivated. I can't wait for you too, to feel the same way by getting more of the right things done.

Mules (Mridu's Rules) For Feeling Awesome
Don't move on to the next Chapter before going through the next short exercise:

1. Take 5-10 minutes right now to time block on your schedule tomorrow for your specific tasks
2. Add a 10-minute block at the end of each day to plan for the next

(Come on over to www.lifeisorganized.com/rightthings for a free resource for all the exercises).

Chapter Four:
Help Thyself or Suffer Endlessly

(Code Letter: "I")

I'm amazed how many people still discover me through my home organization videos. I suppose I shouldn't be given the amount of time and energy I poured into them for years. The longevity of those videos (thank you YouTube and Roku) is priceless for my brand and my business. It was a very hard breakup for me when I finally decided to transition from home organizing to reaching goals and stopped making them.

When I started creating videos, I used my digital camera. *Yes, a camera, people.* It was much better quality than my iPhone 4S at the time. I'd prop it up on a stack of books, jury-rig three large clip-on lamps from Home Depot to my china cabinet, and pray it wasn't overcast on a recording day, so my living room wasn't too dark.

I spent hours editing each video on iMovie (on my refurbished Mac), adding comedic outtakes, step-by-step text, and music. As I got more advanced, I learned about intros and outros, adding click-throughs and subscribe buttons on my YouTube channel. I studied video titles, long tail keywords and descriptions, and spent endless hours on layout redesigns and consistent branding. *...and that was just the video.*

Simultaneously I was writing my weekly blog as an intro to the video content. Creating, editing, posting, keyword tagging, incorporating video screenshots, testing, linking to other blogs, creating calls-to-action, resizing photos, adding borders, formatting, etc.

As you can imagine, this took A LOT of time. I'm not sure I have a real number, like eight or ten hours a week, because I was always working a little bit here and there over the week, but I can say with certainty, it was a big-time stink.

Which left limited time, energy, and focus for all those other things I was supposed to be doing to grow my business and nurture my family.

Things like having real live sales conversations with real live people, building my email list faster than one subscriber every other day, making healthy meals, getting an accounting system in place, and holding all the emotions together at home. *Moms really do deserve a special place in Heaven.*

My husband, a super smart Finance Strategist, would refer to this as Opportunity Cost. By spending time on one thing, you are giving up an opportunity to work on another. *I'm sure there's a much more refined business school definition, but let's drop the formalities, shall we?*

By doing everything myself, guess what my opportunity cost was in terms of a salary? Well if my mathematical equations serve me correctly, one could call it, ummm… half of minimum wage… IF you worked part-time.

I loved creating my vlogs, and I was getting a positive response and great traction, interaction with amazing people, and I finally felt like I was making a true impact. But at the cost of...oh wait, what was that bigger goal? To create a profitable business so I could help more people in the world and pay more than my Target bill. Oh yeah, that one.

As frustrating and painstaking as it was at times to learn how to add graphics, animations, or annotations - there was also something very rewarding about taking on these challenges and coming up with solutions. Then once I figured it out, it was fun to do something that didn't require so much struggle. It was usually at this point that I couldn't even imagine outsourcing this type of work to someone.

Maybe you can relate to some of these reasons, I just couldn't let go.

It takes so long to train someone else. Easier to do just do it myself.

It seems silly to pay someone else for something I'm an expert at. You pay people for things you don't know how to do, not the things you could easily do yourself, right?

I was no stranger to getting help. I'd hired a website and marketing team to design and create my logo, website, and online courses ...but making those videos? Of myself? In my own living room? Come on. That investment of my time was totally worth it.

Until it wasn't.

I look back with 20/20 vision and realize doing it all by myself was as much as an issue with my own pride as it was a procrastination tool. *I'm pretty sneaky like that, aren't I?*

I was putting off getting someone else involved out of fear of the effort I would have to put in and the control I would have to give up.

I was robbing myself the opportunity to grow in other areas.

I was sabotaging my success and ability to reach my goals.

In fact, what I finally realized was the stuff I was really good at, was probably what I should have let go of first.

If you're anything like me, sweet friend, it's time to release the myths. It's time you come clean with the big D. **Delegation.**

Do you have a fear of delegation? Perhaps you've had a bad experience or believe no one can do your job as well as you can. Below are some delegation myths that may be holding you back from getting the support you need to achieve the growth you deserve.

Myth #1: Not enough time to delegate.

- Truthbomb: You don't have time to *not* delegate. The more you get off your plate the more time and energy you will have to focus on strategy, planning, and other priorities that impact your growth. The idea that it's easier to do this myself than to teach someone else, may be true, however, the long-term benefit of eliminating a task will always be greater than the temporary pain of teaching someone else. Ever get your house cleaned? It's divine, isn't it? I still remember closing the door to my Manhattan studio, with a smile ear to ear. I turned around, looked at my perfectly V-patterned vacuum marks and took in a deep breath of lemon scented Pine-Sol euphoria. All I could think to myself was: "Why did I wait so long to get a cleaning service in here?" Once you get the support you really need, you'll wonder why it took you so long to get in the first place.

Myth #2: Other people/staff are not competent enough.

- Truth bomb: It's time to take a trust plunge. When you learn to tap into other people's capabilities, not only will they get more fulfillment from their work, but you will also get a lot more done which will help your business, career, and home life. No doubt it can be scary to give up control and put faith in other people's ability to get the job done. So, don't rely on faith alone. Provide clear, step-by-step directions, talk about expectations, and stay in communication with your people as often as you need to feel comfortable that things are moving along. You will never move past your current state, level, or phase if you don't give yourself space to grow by putting your trust in others.

Myth #3: If you want it done right, you have to do it yourself (aka: Perfectionism).

- Truth bomb: This belief will hold you back and condemn you to perform at an operational level vs. supervisory level. The old "working in your business instead of on your business" adage applies here. The inability to move from doing the job to managing the job is the biggest reason people fail in growing their business and their skills. The natural tendency is to fall back into your comfort zone and start doing rather than delegating. Keep reminding yourself that your job is to lead, not do it yourself. (This is true too if you're a parent leading your kids, family, or home).

Myth #4: People will think you're not on top of things if you delegate to others.

- Truth bomb: Successful people know that great things in their career and life are not achieved by one person, they're achieved by a team. Whether it's your housekeeper, designer, assistant, lawnmower, or accountant, you are stronger together. Enough said.

Myth #5: When you are good at something, you should do it yourself.

- Truth bomb: If you've mastered a skill and can now easily do it, you shouldn't do it yourself because you will not allow yourself room to develop new skills. Delegate it and move on to something else. This myth keeps you trapped in stagnancy which eventually leads to mediocrity, and you my ambitious friend, are capable of much, much more.

Myth #6: I'm already an expert at this. What will someone else bring to the table?

- Truth bomb: This one's a whopper. The idea that your way is the only way, or the best way is holding you hostage to your current state. The truth is, no matter how good you are at folding clothes or editing videos, there's a high likelihood that someone else's fresh perspective could make it better... or more unique...or simpler...or cooler, but you'll never know until you bring someone else in. Don't stand in your own way by excluding someone's new perspective and/or energy.

Get creative.

If you're rolling your eyes thinking I don't have the money or the resources to go out and invest in a writer, blogger, assistant, marketer, sitter, housekeeper, errand runner, or dog walker, think again.

If you are serious about making changes in your career, life, and relationships, you will figure out a way to get the help you really need. Even if it's for just two hours a week.

When my boys were young, ages three and six, my hubby and I threw a Valentine's Party. In case you don't know, I have a fetish with theme parties as well as adult party games. So, this was the perfect occasion to bring my two obsessions together.

Full on red and pink decor, table covered in Valentine delights with chocolate fondue and red velvet cupcakes, and to top it off, chocolate raspberry martinis. Games were rated 21 and older, adorned with his and her matching underwear, amongst the mix of prizes. In a nutshell, my dream party.

Having entertained a lot in the past we knew how to bring the many pieces of the experience together. Clean the house, prepare the food, put up the decorations, organize the games, get our kids to sleep...

As far as the kids were concerned, my first thought was to hire a sitter for the night to keep them in their rooms and put them to sleep, so we could focus on our guests and entertaining, but my hubby came up with the most brilliant idea. If our goal was to have a fun and memorable night with our friends, what was it that we really needed help with? The biggest, most dreaded piece in this whole experience.

The morning after.

Yup, waking up at 6:00 a.m. for the kids after weeks of planning, a day of preparation, and a night of martini's, and add all that post-party cleaning. Now that was going to be painful!

That's where the brilliant idea came into play. We were pretty sure we could get the kids to mostly stay upstairs and even get them to sleep with the help of some of friendly bribing techniques... the iPad and gifts they could open first thing in the morning if they went to bed on time. ...*give it up for The Dollar Store.* We'd keep them wrapped and at the foot of their bed for good behavior.

Instead of spending the $60 on four hours on a sitter at night, we had her come in at 6:00 a.m. the next day so she could keep the kids entertained and happy until 9:00 a.m. *When you have young kids, staying in bed until 9:00 a.m. is a dream, am I right?!* We tacked on two more hours and from 9:00 a.m. - 11:00 a.m. she agreed to wash and dry all our platters and dishes from the night before.

It. Was. Amazing.

Not only the time we saved doing tasks we dreaded but even more rewarding was the alleviation of mental stress and energy.

The weight of only getting a few hours of sleep to take on two energetic and demanding boys coupled with an upside-down house simply... vanished. With a little creativity, we reallocated our resources and used them where we could benefit from them the most.

You always have opportunities for creativity. Here are some examples:

- You could barter services. *I'll help you with your site redesign if you help me with my accounting.*

    - **Mental stress alleviated:** Stop stressing out about the fact that I'm not tracking my income and expenses.

- You could start with personal time. *Clean my house for four hours every other week.*

    - **Mental stress alleviated:** Stop arguing with my spouse about whose turn it is to scrub the toilets.

- You could hire a high school or college student for $10-$15 an hour who is happy to make extra money: *Input these email addresses and names I collected into my database.*

    - **Mental stress alleviated:** Stop procrastinating this simple, yet really important task. *I can't build a relationship with these interested folks until they're in my system.*

If your wheels are starting to spin, awesome. That's exactly where you should be. Dreaming of all the little tasks and the creative ways you could free up your own time and mental energy.

Imagining ways to offload the big projects to create more space in your calendar and ignite creative and strategic ideas in your brain.

Without investing in the help you need, you will never move beyond where you are. If you're cool with the status of your income, business growth, social life, relationships, and personal development, by all means, don't invest in yourself.

Truth bomb: If you're looking to get to the next level, a bump in your number of clients, the depth of your friendships and intimacy, the commitment to your health and wellness, please don't fool or convince yourself into believing that you can do it all.

One of the simplest ways I've thought about what tasks to get help with is to follow Jenny Blake's six T's, (published on HBR.com), to determine what tasks make the most sense to offload. Even if you're not sure yet who to delegate to, or even how, start by capturing the what. Then watch as your mind magically starts creating solutions for next steps from that new perspective of space and self-awareness.

1. **Tiny:** Tasks that are so small they seem inconsequential to tackle, but they add up. They are never important or urgent, and even if they only take a few minutes they end up taking you out of the flow of more strategic

work. For example, registering for an event, adding it to your calendar, and booking the hotel and flight. On their own each of these tasks may not take much time, but taken together, they all add up.

2. **Tedious:** Tasks that are relatively simple probably are not the best use of your time. Very straightforward tasks can (and should) be handled by anyone but you. For example, manually inputting a 100-item list into a spreadsheet and color-coding it or wrapping gifts and sending out holiday cards.

3. **Time-consuming:** Tasks that, although they may be important and even somewhat complex, are time-consuming but you can easily step in when the task is 80% complete and give approval, oversight and/or direction on next steps. For example, giving feedback and final approval of a newsletter layout or closet re-organization.

4. **Teachable:** Tasks that, although complicated-seeming at first and possibly comprising several smaller subtasks, can be translated into a system and passed along, with you still providing quality checks and final approval. For example, teaching one of your direct reports how to draft and deliver the presentation for a monthly meeting.

5. **Terrible at:** Tasks that not only do not fall into your strengths but an area where you feel unequipped. For example, the visual design of

those PowerPoint slides for the team meeting or hiring a landscaper to manage your yard and garden.

6. **Time sensitive:** Tasks that are time-sensitive but compete with other priorities. For example, leaving your iPad on the plane after a flight and working to recover it by calling customer service (which takes an hour!)

One effective way to determine what to delegate is checking in frequently to examine what's on your plate and ask: What can you and only you do? How can you delegate the rest?

Will there be bumps along the way while you're training, advising, or guiding your new-found assistance? Of course, there will. In fact, chances are the first assistant, cat groomer, or laundry folder won't do things the way you wished.

They'll mess up the system, they'll leave out a step, they'll be inconsistent with your brand, they'll put the poop diapers in the kitchen trash and leave it there. *Ugh!*

You will be frustrated at times. Amused at other times. Exasperated too.

Through your experience, you'll learn to give better directions, create greater collaboration, and identify personality types that do and don't work for you.

If you're open-minded and aware that perhaps everything you do your way isn't always the best way and that other people can bring fresh and exciting perspectives, you'll also learn to compromise and mold your expectations.

In the very act of getting help, you will grow as a human, leader, manager, parent, and friend.

<u>You will unburden yourself of great anxiety and stress.</u> Instead of crowding out your current ideas by desperately trying to squish in new ones, you will have mental space for new, big ideas, bursting with energy you never had the room for before. These thoughts will connect to other thoughts and before you know, you'll be one big idea generating think tank.

<u>You will be more focused.</u> When you can drop the nagging feeling of everything you should be doing and ditch the overwhelming reminders of everything you're not doing, you will allow yourself to focus on what really matters.

If you know someone else is handling the 32 steps it takes to upload your blog and post it across five different social media platforms, you can focus on providing the best damn information that will have your readers begging for more.

If you know someone else is picking up your dry cleaning, making your CVS returns, and chauffeuring your kids to and from soccer practice, you can focus on setting up your automatic bill pay and creating a meal plan so your home runs like a turnkey system.

<u>You will be more successful.</u> Investing in help multiplies your results by improving the quality and quantity of your results, and better results will influence and determine your income, position, and level of personal satisfaction in your work and life.

On the other overwhelming hand, if all results are dependent on you, you will never grow or scale.

As an effective leader, business owner, parent, family member, supervisor, or manager, you have to leave time in your day and life for planning, strategy, and vision. If you're stuck in the day to day monotonous, time-consuming, life sucking and unchallenging tasks and chores, you have no time or headspace to think bigger picture.

The truth is, the do it all myself mentality leads to exhaustion, inefficiency, and low productivity.

Now that I've beat you over the head with idea of investing in some help, *I tend to do that when I'm passionate about something*, let's talk briefly about the "How?"

Whether you're bartering services, hiring a virtual assistant, or bringing on your twentieth employee, there is a right way and a wrong way to get help.

The Wrong Way:

I have a need. You have an expertise. Here's what I want done. Either do this task the way I've done it in the past (see this thing here?) or use your best judgment and do it your way (as long as it turns out exactly the way I like it done).

Example.

Me: (talking to my son): Can you please load the dishwasher?

Krishin: How do I do that, mom?

Me: Just pick up the dishes and put them in. You've seen me do it a million times.

Krishin: I don't know how.

Me: (starting to get irritated). Just get them from the sink and put them in. It's no big deal.

Krishin: Ok, whatever mom. (*clank, crash, goop, thump, clunk*)

Me: What are you doing?!

Krishin: What you told me to do. Putting the dishes in.

Me: You have to rinse them first. They don't clean themselves! Why are the mugs on the bottom? You don't put the bowls and plates on the same side, you'll barely get five dishes in. Etc. Etc. Etc.

Krishin: (screaming) I told you I didn't know how to do them!

Me: (biting my tongue and thinking, "How is this my child? Really, is it so hard?)

Me an hour later.

I am an awful mom. I couldn't have handled that any worse! Of course, he doesn't know how to load the dishwasher. I've never taught him.

This is how most help is brought in, it doesn't work out and then we blame the person.

He just couldn't handle the job.

She didn't know how to make the batter right.

He was too caught up in design.

She would always show up in a shirt cut waaaaay too low.

He wouldn't write anything down.

She text in front of a client.

He always lets something fall through the cracks.

She let the kids play video games all night long!

Without crystal clear expectations and step-by-step directions, you need to take a good hard look at your process, (and lack thereof), before placing the blame on someone else.

Here are ways I've found most effective when hiring a housekeeper to a graphic designer.

1. Match the person to the job: Not everyone is the right fit for every job. Set your team up for success by being aware of matching specific skill sets or areas of growth for specific requests. My sitter who can make a crumpled cardboard box look like a luxurious welcome basket will likely be super helpful with planning the holiday party, but probably not the best bet for updating my accounting system.

2. Describe the benefit: Acknowledge not only their role but also how completing this task or project will benefit them. Making someone feel needed, included, and part of the team builds their skill set, confidence, and helps them do a better job, rather than simply telling them what to do. At the end of the day, everyone wants to know, "What's in it for me?" and "Why should I care?"

   o Sure, Jeff can enter the email names and addresses. Once he knows that, as those names become clients, your company helps more people, makes more money, and he gets a raise. Now Jeff is thinking about where he can get even more names to add to that list.

3. Provide clear direction: Set your team member up for success by giving them the tools they need. Create guidelines or other documentation that clearly lays out all their steps. This will not only help them succeed

but will give you the confidence you need to delegate the task.

Let's talk some truth here before we move on. Clear direction takes thought and time. Yes, it might be easier to just do it yourself than to train someone else, but putting in the training time upfront will save you hours upon hours in the future. This is a necessary step but also one that you are most likely to procrastinate. Here are some easy ways to take the pain out of this step.

- o Use checklists. Remember those video blogs I told you about - that I used to do all by myself? In my mind, I thought I might be doing 20-25 steps from start to finish to get that out every week. When I actually broke down each step (in a simple checklist format), it turned out I was doing over 64 steps each time. *Lord have mercy, no wonder I didn't have time for anything else.* Rather than write out a 10-page Word document, I simply had checklists for the four different parts of the projects: Video, Blog, Photography, and Social Media. Don't overthink it. Just start writing down each step as you go through a process, so you have it in a checklist for someone else to do.

o   Use video. This training tool is so highly underused and underrated. Imagine teaching someone how to input hundreds of names into your database or CRM system, or how to upload a new workshop, or revise your checkout cart. There are a lot of little buttons to press, dropdowns, options to check off, menus to scroll through, and screens to bypass. What if you could walk someone through it right on your screen, as if they were sitting right next to you, so you didn't have to painfully create the step-by-step document? You can record your screen with simple tools like Zoom. This has been a lifesaver for me for technical training on both the giving and receiving end.

4.   <u>Ask for specific results:</u> The more specific and measurable results people can accomplish, the happier and more motivated they will be. For example, if you hire someone for data entry, they might take their time entering one line at a time, while getting distracted by their phone every couple of minutes. When you tell them to reach 150 entries within the next two hours, they're more likely to put away their phone after the fourth Snapchat alert in order to meet the expectation. They might even come up with a more efficient or creative way to enter the information to ensure they hit the deadline.

5. Encourage participation and discussion: Let your team, new hire, assistant, or colleague know you are always available for questions or discussions. People will be more vested in you and their results as well as be more creative when they can count on open lines of communication and encouragement. I cannot stress this enough. Be approachable. Invite discussions. Smile. Laugh. It will do your teamwork good.

6. Leave the person alone: Nobody wants to be micromanaged. *"Please stand over my shoulder and shake your head in disapproval as I work my way through this,"* said no one ever. People will demonstrate greater loyalty, commitment, and dedication to you when they feel a sense of ownership and personal empowerment. Treat them with respect and let them try, and perhaps even fail, on their own. Don't overcrowd their space or sense of control, unless of course, they are headed full speed into quicksand, in which case, throw a big, fat, neon orange lifesaver around them and reel them in before they sink.

7. Appreciate and recognize: When the job is complete, express your appreciation. Like, with words. Don't overlook two powerful ones: *"Thank You."* Gratitude goes a long way in job satisfaction and personal motivation, but here's the whopper, if the job is *not* done the way you would have wished, still show gratitude. I know, it's not always

easy, but be thankful for the effort that was put it, along with constructive feedback for future improvements. *Ain't nobody on this earth who doesn't want to feel valued.* Speaking of which, if you have the opportunity to express recognition publicly, take advantage of it. Let your team members know the great work that Josh did on formatting the product images or Cheryl did catching the grammatical error on the proposal. People who feel appreciated are more positive about themselves, their ability to contribute, and are potentially the best people to support you.

If you can't delegate effectively, you can't fulfill your potential. Invest in help, whether it be small and mighty, or big and powerful. People who accomplish more and consistently feel good about what they get done, use their time and resources in the most effective way possible to get the maximum leverage.

That's just a fancy way of saying: *"If you want to feel valued and really awesome at the end of each day, get the support you need to get you there."*

Mules (Mridu's Rules) For Living to Your Potential

Don't move on to the next Chapter before going through the next short exercise:

List 3 specific tasks you know you should be getting help with or delegating entirely. (This can be personal or professional).

1. _____

2. _____

3. _____

Now pick one of them and commit to your immediate next steps to make it happen.

1. _____

2. _____

3. _____

(Come on over to www.lifeisorganized.com/rightthings for a free resource for all the exercises).

Chapter Five:
Say It Loud and Proud

(Code Letter: "O")

A couple years ago I worked with a client, Tessa, who is super smart. Like, ivy league college smart. Like, Ph.D smart. Like, I'm the boss of my own dentistry practice smart.

Tack on two beautiful and sassy girls and a husband who traveled a lot, she was one of those Superwomen you admired from afar.

"I bet her house is spotless."

"How does she always look like that?"

"Did she bake those brownies herself?"

Then, when you found out she was on three Boards, Classroom Mom, and actively involved in her church, girrrrl, she radiated untouchable mode. There's no way I could reach that level, and her always *Steady Eddy* composure? It was downright unnatural.

Yet, I wasn't surprised when she contacted me about coaching, that the unmistakable "But..." was lurking in the background. *"I'm doing so great, really things are just awesome...But..."*

"My business is a mess! I'm so behind on my invoices and insurance claims, I'm far behind in getting paid. I'm embarrassed to be double booking or missing

appointments and regularly misplacing files. My younger daughter was just diagnosed with A.D.D. My house is overloaded, and overwhelming..." ...and no surprise, things with her hubby weren't as blissful as they seemed.

For the seemingly put together CEO, mom, and wife, she was just as confused and stressed out as the rest of us. Was it the kids? The house? The business? The marriage?

Certainly, a little of all of it. It *is* a lot to handle, but after a deeper dive into her behaviors and actions, it was clear that there was another, more formidable power at play.

Tessa couldn't say No. Like ever.

Bake sale? *Yes.*

Church night? *Sign me up.*

Grab my dry cleaning? *Of course!*

Join the committee? *With pleasure.*

I don't want to eat that mom. *What else can I whip up for you dear?*

Yes, ma'am. Yes, sir. Yes, please. Yes, thank you. Yes-siree-bob! Yes, yes, yes, yes, yes, yes, yes!

She was what you might call a People Pleaser. A Giver. A Helper.

aka: A really good woman with a really big heart.

Unfortunately, her desire to please and her inability to say "No", left her burdened with too many places to be, too many things to do, and too many commitments to tend to.

Which meant her big priorities: kids, biz, hubby, and home, almost always took the backseat to her overcommitted schedule and calendar. Simply stretched too thin, Tessa felt like she wasn't doing anything in particularly well in her life.

Drowning in confusion, overloaded with next steps, follow-ups, bake sales, meeting recaps, girl scout meetings, annual retreats, and I don't even know why I'm at this event, she wasn't feeling as awesome as she hoped all the "yeses" would make her feel.

"I feel like a fraud. Everyone thinks I have it all together, and really, I'm barely keeping my head above water. I feel like I'm in demand every second I'm awake and it makes me want to cry."

Whoa. Not a fun and rewarding way to live. Especially when you are giving, giving, giving so much. Perhaps that was the problem. Perhaps, she was giving too much?

I hadn't uncovered the great unknown. She knew deep down that her lack of boundaries was causing her extreme anxiety. Even though she loved the fact that she accomplished a lot, it was the risk of constantly feeling unsatisfied and always behind. Tessa definitely didn't have time to think about a plan or about how to change it.

If this sounds at all eerily familiar, listen up sweet friend! For every "Yes" you say, you say "No" to someone or something else.

Yes, to coaching the soccer team, means *No* to making meals those nights.

Yes, to the Director of Events position, means *No* to Chairing the charity you love.

Yes, to sponsoring the Music Gala, means *No* to getting the rest you need.

Yes, to taking on another project, means *No* to watching a movie with the kids Friday night.

Yes, to the partnership, means *No* to finally writing your book.

Yes, to another party, means *No* to organizing your home.

Truth bomb: To take control of your time and goals and feel truly accomplished at the end of each day, you have to practice saying "No." ...*or at the very least, "Not now please".*

Before you get in a tizzy about me telling you to say "No" to helping your church or school or work committee, hold onto your tighty-whities and let me explain. I'm not suggesting you always say "No", rather be thoughtful about when you say "Yes".

The next time you accept, nod, shake on, or sign another commitment ask yourself these three questions:

1. What else do I currently have going on?

2. Do I have the time, space, and energy to take this on (and do it well)?

3. By taking this on, will I still have the time and space I need for my big priorities?

Take the couple of minutes to process it, think it through and make an intentional decision. It helps to understand your own long-term goals first. Those big priorities of yours). This way, you can say yes to opportunities that most reflect your values.

We live in a "yes" culture, where it's expected that the person who is the go-getter says "yes" to everything is the one that will get ahead or be more liked. Meanwhile, it's the people who learn to say "no" that have more meaningful relationships and careers that really take off.

We're sometimes afraid to say "no" because we fear missing out. We want to take on new opportunities and adventures, so we say "yes" to everything instead, but all of those yes' can lead to burnout.

Another way we continue to "yes", without even knowing it, is by reacting to every beep, ding, ping, alert, ringtone, email, instant message, Facebook message, text, call, voicemail, CRM notification, or Tweet. By responding, we are constantly saying "yes" to other people's demands, giving up our personal power and control.

For such a tiny word, "no" is profoundly liberating. When you decide, "this does not warrant my immediate attention, or this is counterproductive and I'm not doing this" you embrace your intuition.

How many times have you thought "why did I just say yes to that?" about two seconds after you did, or more likely, as you were saying "yes", you've heard that little voice in your head saying *"Noooooo! You really shouldn't be taking this on right now."* Trust your gut—your brain will thank you.

The solution

The simplest way I've learned to say "no" is to communicate. People will eventually respect you for taking control of your time and needs. Saying "no" shows you have a vision, a plan, and an opinion. It gives you authority.

By letting people know your needs, challenges, deadlines, or other commitments you not only begin to eliminate distractions, but you also stop feeling inclined to people please all the time.

Get more comfortable with saying "No." First, practice it when the stakes are low. For example, when a cashier asks you if you want the two-for-one chocolates as you check out, say "No thank you." Then walk away and give yourself a virtual pat on the back. "This girl can say no!"

It's a lot easier to be assertive with a stranger selling you something than it is when your colleague asks you to join her after work for drinks, while you really should be finishing your expense reports from last quarter. Get comfortable with your assertiveness when it's easy, so you'll be prepared when there's more pressure.

Key takeaway: Saying "no", shows you're in control of the situation, and that you have integrity in your personal and professional value. It also makes you feel really, really good about yourself.

Don't overcompensate

When you're first trying on "no" for a size, you'll be tempted to explain why because you don't want the person requesting your help to think you're so awful you'd say "no" for no reason at all. Chances are it will be a long, drawn out, unnecessarily detailed explanation, that leaves room for more questions, discussions, and guilt, rather than put the request to bed.

"Hey Nancy, any chance you could drive me to the airport on Friday after work?"

"I'd really love to Roger. You know I'm always happy to help, but my kids get out of school at 3:30 on Friday. I have to get my younger one to soccer practice by 4 o'clock. While he's there I hop onto I-440 in a mad dash to catch the end of my daughter's tennis match. I could possibly take you after that, but I'm worried that with all the traffic I won't get back in time to get my son by 5:30, home by 6:00, and then across town to make it out for dinner plans at 7 o'clock. I'm really sorry. If anything changes, I'll let

you know. What time do you get back on Sunday? Maybe I could pick you up then?"

"Uh...no problem Nancy. I'll just call an Uber."

The recipient of your explanation vomit is probably, even more, overwhelmed thinking about how hectic and stressed your life is in addition to their problem of getting to the airport.

Let's try that scenario again.

"Hey Nancy, any chance you could drive me to the airport on Friday after work?"

"Sorry, Roger, I have plans. Maybe next time."

Everyone feels at ease, no added drama, explanations, or confusion about the outcome.

It helps to reverse the situation. If someone asked YOU for help, and they politely and respectfully said *"No, I can't."*, would you assume they're declining because they don't like you? They're scared of you? They don't like polka-dotted shirts? Probably not.

In fact, you might not think anything about it, other than, "Who else can I ask to help me solve this problem?"

That said, providing a "no" without context can seem harsh. Add a few words like, *"No, I'm not able to,"* or *"No, I don't have time right now."* or *"No, it's not a good time for me."* or *"No, I already have plans."* Feel free to throw in a, *"Thank you for asking/thinking of me.*" if you feel like adding an extra scoop of politeness.

Either way, the idea is to avoid explanations and simply give context. Too much information will only lead to problems and demonstrate that you feel guilty about saying no.

It's also easier to say "no" when you know exactly how to say it, so come up with a few phrases for different situations.

"No, I'm already committed in three other organizations." for your friend at The Chamber of Commerce.

"No, I don't go out during the week." for co-workers who want to go on a drinking binge on a Tuesday night.

When you have these phrases ready, you don't have to waste time thinking of an excuse or stuttering over your words. Saying "no" is like a muscle. The more you use it, the easier it becomes to use it.

Don't get addicted to no.

There's one more thing you should always remember: don't remove "yes" from your vocabulary. Once you start to feel comfortable with saying "no" more regularly and enjoy the free time you've regained in your life, you'll probably be more inclined to say it whenever something you don't want to do arises.

Unfortunately, you're sometimes going to have to do things you don't want to do. Most people don't enjoy cleaning, but you can't say "no" to doing the dishes forever. You also may want to help your friends move even though it's not your ideal way to spend a Saturday. These are situations you're likely aware of, but it's important to keep them in mind. Keep your "no's" and "yeses" balanced out.

What about when you can't say no?

When your boss, supervisor, or well-paying client asks you to take on another project or handle another situation, you can't simply say "no." Unless getting reprimanded and perhaps even fired, is your kind of thing.

It also does not suffice to say, *"No, thank you, Marla, I have enough on my plate right now."* Try that out next time your client delivers more business for you.

So, what do you say? How do you create and maintain boundaries?

When it comes to being an effective leader and taking control of your time, I've found it is still best to communicate, and by communicate, please don't take on the form of whining, complaining, or embarking on a compulsive twitch every time you think about how much you have going on.

Talk to your people. Include them on the decision making. Assure that everyone is on the same page. Prioritize together.

Does your boss, supervisor, client, or spouse know everything that's on your plate all the time? Of course not. Just like you don't know what's on theirs. When you are receiving requests and demands it's in everybody's best interest to understand the implications and reset the expectations.

In business, this might translate to your client or manager emailing you details on a new social media campaign to be delivered in four days. Your head swells and vision goes blurry as you try to process when, where, and how you will add this to your already overflowing sink full of projects, follow-ups, and tasks. Your immediate reaction might be to agree, without question, as you work from a place of integrity and not complaint.

Now the new you arises, the you that does what she can to take control of her time, that uses time language, that embeds in her mind that the worse that can happen is that nothing changes, and I won't be any worse than I am now.

You pick up the phone, call your busy client, and boldly muster up the courage to say:

"Barb, I got your email about the new social media campaign. It sounds like an awesome project, and I'm happy you asked me to be a part of it." Pause while you take a deep inhale. *"I just want to confirm that this takes precedence over the editorial calendar which you wanted just the day before? Both take equal time, so if I work on the calendar first, it won't be possible to get the campaign buttoned up by Friday."* Aaaaaaand breathe again.

Pause on the other line. *"Well, actually now that you brought it up, the editorial calendar can wait. The social media campaign is more important."*

"Great. So, I'll go ahead and put my resources to the social media campaign and make sure to have that over to you by Friday. As soon as that's complete, I'll jump back on the editorial calendar. That's helpful, thanks for your time."

Moral of the story: <u>Don't prioritize other people's agendas by yourself.</u> If you're truly conflicted on time and resources (or simply don't have enough of either) have a conversation about it with the person or people making the as to prioritize and determine next steps together.

Benefits of these conversations:

- It avoids any misinterpretation of what the priorities are

- It diffuses awkward conversations later

- It stops putting all the pressure on you to figure it all out or read other people's minds

- It fosters partnership and collaboration (valuable tools for an effective leader)

- It sets expectations for results

- It gives you clarity and makes you feel successful

- It lets you breathe again and stop breaking out in hives

Here are other ways to respond as well:

"I'd love to do this right now! Just so you know, I'll need to delay those expense reimbursements I was working on for you."

"Yes, count me in! I want to do this project really well. Is there anyone else we call in to help ensure it's a success?"

"I'd love to jump in and help, but I have a lot on my plate right now. Can we discuss how to make this work?"

Working together to come up with a game plan is far more effective, productive, and rewarding than drowning in a puddle of sweat, overwhelmed with anxiety, taking on the stress by yourself.

Sure, you could try to just power through all of the projects or tasks, but you probably know that's neither the best nor the most professional option. Pushing back on a request from your boss or client can be intimidating (especially if you work for someone who's not the most receptive to answers outside of *"Of course! When would you like it completed?"*). The truth is, it's significantly better than setting yourself up to fail.

Get your point across without actually using the word "no." In fact, say the opposite. *"Yes, I can! Let's just figure out how."* With this strategy, you are always viewed as a positive team player and partner, which is a home run because nobody wants to work with Debbie Downer.

There's another common scenario that comes up at work, and even at home, that totally stress out my clients. Chatty Charlie.

You see him coming a mile away. *Doesn't he ever have any work to do? Can't he see I have my headphones on?*

If you work at home like I do, this could be your friend, or mom, who loves calling smack in the middle of the day and chats with you like you are a lady of leisure, sitting at home without a care in the world. *Seriously ma, I know you just got back from bridge and are all hot and bothered by the stale crackers they served, but I'm trying to run a business here.*

About three minutes into the conversation you're distracted by seven more emails that have popped up on your screen, two minutes later you feel your heart rate rising as you watch the time dwindle away on your clock and three more minutes later you are in full on agitation mode. "When are they going to wrap this up?!"

Guess what? Your mom, friend, colleague, boss, or partner cannot read your mind (and in some cases, your very obvious body language). How do you handle this situation? You guessed it. Use your "time" language. Own. Your. Voice.

In the words of someone great: *Ain't nobody gonna respect your time unless you do.*

Which means it's up to you to own your voice, use your words and take control of the situation before it gets out of hand. Here are some simple reactions in these types of situations:

"I'm in the middle of something I need to focus on. Could you check back in about 45 minutes?"

"Sorry, I'm under a tight deadline. Could we chat at lunch?"

"I'm so behind on my stuff right now. Let's pick this up later, okay?"

"If this will truly take two minutes or less, I can talk right now. Otherwise, let's look at our calendars to schedule time to speak."

How about the "straightforward, couldn't be any more transparent approach":

"I'm trying to stay more focused and manage my time better, which means I have to stay on track. Can we talk later?"

If someone gave you any of those responses when you wanted to talk to them unannounced, would you be offended? Uh, no. You'd probably say something along the lines of, *"Sure, no problem." "Of course!" "I totally understand."*

The only reason you might feel insecure about saying any of those responses is because you haven't said them before. Not because they are mean or disingenuous or disrespectful.

Which means you just need to practice. Have your responses written down, role play with a friend, or practice in front of the mirror. Get used to being in the driver's seat by empowering yourself with the tools to be in control.

You have a God-given powerful tool to take control of your time, get more done, and feel more accomplished at the end of each day. Use your voice, with honesty and respect, and wrangle in those interruptions before *they* control YOU.

Take control of your meetings

You know those days when you have back-to-back meetings or appointments and you get back to your office only to find 332 unread emails, 27 voicemails, and a stack of papers awaiting your response? Two words to sum this up: Over. Whelming.

It's hard enough to take a breath on days like that and have some sense of composure or preparedness for each meeting. It's even more frustrating and panic-inducing when the meetings you had went longer than scheduled.

All because Betty spent 15 minutes talking about her dog eating a bag of chips.

...or because everyone huddled around Dave's phone, oohing and aahing over photos of the ponies at his three year old's birthday party.

...or because Run-It-Off-The-Rails Rita took every opportunity to tell a story and get off topic.

...or because Make-A-Point-Already Michael took fourteen minutes to essentially say, "I agree."

Meanwhile, you're feeling an anxiety attack come on as you're losing count of all the things you need to get done by the end of the day.

Meeting heavy cultures have become the norm. In addition to adding more and more on, it seems they're becoming increasingly inefficient. More people, more opinions, more fluff, more personal stories, more time wasted.

Since we're on the topic of owning your voice I thought it would be appropriate to spend a few minutes on speaking up and taking control of meetings. Yes, it *is* possible.

Imagine if you walked into each meeting with a clear purpose, kept attendees on track (and on time), and left knowing exactly what everyone was responsible for, by when.

I think that's how meetings were held back in the old days. You know, before smartphones and social media and working 12 hours a day was standard. The good old-fashioned days when Ginny called a meeting with Sam to figure out the venue for the summer picnic. They met for 15 minutes, brainstormed three places, and called them all by the next day.

Those were the days. Meetings with a real purpose and an actual result.

Good news. You can get the old days back. Here are two steps to make it happen:

1. Create an agenda

2. Use your voice

If you just saw the word "agenda" and are thinking, *"Please woman, do not give me one more thing to do!"* read on.

Unlike the old days, I'm not talking about creating a Word document on company letterhead, pondering over points and sub-points, and arriving late to your meeting because you were fighting with the copy machine.

Instead, think three short bullet points to be included in your meeting request. No formatting. No copies. No drama. Very little extra work for a very big result.

In the meeting description, simply add 3-5 bullet points on what you'll specifically be discussing.

Listen up. Here's where the magic happens. This next tiny tweak can be the difference of your thirty-minute meeting going on for forty-five or walking out with all three points resolved instead of one.

Add a time to each point. (Yes, you Communication Sleuth, this is another effective way to use your time language).

Check out this bad boy agenda below, right in the description of the meeting you're scheduling.

Meeting Name: Spring Social Media Campaign Kick Off

Agenda:

- Review client background document: *10 minutes*

- Assign roles and responsibilities: *15 minutes*

- Recap next steps and timeline: *5 minutes*

There it is. Done. With this forty-second exercise you've set everyone's expectations for the meeting, including your own. By the way, I do this even when I have meetings with myself, like:

9:30 - 10:00 Decide on e-book name

- Brainstorm ideas: 20 minutes

- Narrow down to three: 5 minutes

- Pick one and move on!: 5 minutes

It's amazing what you can accomplish when you give yourself or others boundaries around time.

Ok, so step one recap. Do not schedule any more team meetings, family meetings, self-meetings, prospect meetings, or client meetings without a simple three-point agenda with time boundaries. Kapeesh?

This is not difficult and nowhere near rocket science. If you're committed to getting the right things done in your day, feeling accomplished...and just moving on with things already, you'll put this easy-peasy tip into effect pronto.

Let's move onto Step Two. Back to using your beautiful voice. Own your voice DURING the meeting. Dominating Dave or Rambling Rachel will get your meeting so off track that you'll forget what the purpose of getting together was so it's up to you to take control through verbal communication. Here are some ways to make it happen:

1. **Start on time.**

    a. On time doesn't mean five minutes after the start time. It means on time. If someone is consistently late and they see you're well into the meeting by the time they walk or call in, chances are by the third meeting with you, they'll be on time. Call the meeting to start on time.

2. **Take the first minute to welcome your guests, confirm the agenda and set the ground rules.**

    a. *"Thanks for being here, on time, to discuss the social media strategy for next quarter. We have 60 minutes to get through this, so please put your phones on vibrate and away, turn off your email and let's jump right in so* we can wrap up on time. We're going to spend the first 15 minutes going through Q1 results, 25 minutes discussing changes for Q2, 15 minutes to discuss roles and responsibilities, and the last 5 minutes to make sure we're all clear on next steps. If we're getting off track and spending too much time on a point, I'll let you know we need to move on and will ask you to summarize. Sound good? Great. Let's get going."

3. **Use your time language throughout the meeting to keep everyone on track.**

   a. As the organizer of the meeting, it is up to YOU to take charge. Here are some of my favorite ways to keep everyone aware of the time and stay on track without looking like a time Nazi:

   - *"Just want to remind everyone we're at our halfway point..."*

   - *'In the interest of getting everyone heard, we'll have to move on to the next point, Bill..."*

   - *"With our remaining 15 minutes, I suggest we focus on..."*

   - *"That sounds like a great discussion for another meeting. I'll make a note to schedule a follow-up."*

- *"I'm going to set a five-minute timer for our remaining four points…"* (Do not be afraid to use your timer! Your nerdiness will pay off big time when you come out of your meeting with results and clear next steps)

- *"We have three minutes left, so let's recap."* (Always end your meetings with a recap so there is absolutely no confusion about who is responsible for what, by when).

With a few simple phrases, you can wrangle in long-winded ramblers and off-point storytellers that sabotage meetings and throw them off course.

Like any skill, this takes practice. I suggest you have a few phrases ready before your next meeting (even if you're not the one leading it). A leader will appreciate your ability to bring semblance to the plan and order to the chaos.

We build fences around our yards, so our kids and pets are protected. We put passwords on our information, so our identities are protected. We set limits on our credit cards, so our finances are protected.

We use boundaries in all areas of our lives. Yet, when it comes to our own personal boundaries, we struggle with creating them and feel uncomfortable sticking to them.

Our most valuable resource, our time, deserves to be protected, cared for, and even coveted. When it comes to reaching our goals and making an impact in our homes, careers, families, communities, and world, time is our most precious gift.

Your words are powerful. Your voice is magnificent. Using your voice can be the difference between reacting to emails, tweets, and posts for hours on end to putting your head down, getting in the zone, and finally getting that proposal out the door.

You, my mighty friend, are a time warrior. You are destined to achieve big, bold, beautiful things. Use your voice, conquer the world, and feel accomplished by getting the right things done.

MULES (Mridu's Rules) For Feeling Empowered
Do not move onto the next Chapter before filling out the below:

Write a word for word script you will practice and be armed with the next time you are asked to take on a <u>personal</u> commitment you know you shouldn't accept right now.

_____

_____

_____

Write a word for word script you will practice and be armed with the next time you are asked to take on a professional commitment you know you shouldn't accept right now.

_____

_____

_____

Create three bullet points for an upcoming meeting you already have scheduled or need to schedule.

_____

_____

_____

(Come on over to www.lifeisorganized.com/rightthings for a free resource for all the exercises).

Chapter Six:
If You're Going Mental

(Code Letter: "N")

Diana, a client I coached, was managing two businesses. A family inherited jam store and a Rodan & Fields (skincare) business. Along with her three dogs and two chickens, she also owned a countryside property with three units that she maintained for Airbnb customers. After our first session, it was clear that her goal was to run things more efficiently to make more money in all her pursuits. Not to mention have time and space to enjoy her life that she'd been working so hard to build up.

We started working in depth on some of the principles and habits we've covered in this book. Avoiding distractions, blocking her time, and creating boundaries.

One day I was checking in on her, (I do that a lot with my clients), and she was on what felt like the verge of a nervous breakdown. Amidst home renovations, preparing for or rather freaking out about a skincare class she was teaching a week later, a church event she was helping with, friends coming in town, a difficult client, and a slower than usual month, she sounded frantic, overwhelmed, and most certainly like she could use a drink. Since I didn't think offering a cold stiff one would be the best recommendation as a coach, I suggested she write it all down.

"Write what down?" sounding totally confused.

"Write it all down. All of it. Everything that is in your head. Every to-do, task, next step, thought, project, all of it. Get it out of your head and onto paper and send it to me."

"Why? I just told you everything I have going on," she quickly responded.

"You're going to make it much harder on yourself trying to figure out your priorities when it's all living in your head. Trust me on this one."

With so much hesitancy "Ok, whatever you say." Massive eye rolling on the other end.

About an hour later I received an email from Diana with an attachment marked "My List."

I opened it up and I kid you not, it was four and a half pages long. Single typed. Wow, those are a lot of thoughts.

"How does that feel?"

"Weirdly good. Feels good to get it out of my head but scary to see it all on paper."

"Perfect, that means you did it right. Now, if you could only pick three of those tasks that you could move on today, what would they be?"

"Well, three are easy. Send an email to market my class next week, pick out the light for my renovations, and contact a few prospects I met at an event yesterday."

"Great. Get to it." I responded. "Just like that. Don't overthink. Don't get mesmerized and paralyzed by the rest of the list. Just take action on one of those three tasks. Like now, please."

I'm happy to report that I received five (not three) thumbs up emoji's over the course of the day, one for every task Diana completed. With everything out of her head and a focus on just a few tasks, she squashed paralysis and got moving on her to-do's.

I'm willing to bet you have endless thoughts too.

Not only is your business brain always charged with ideas, but your commitments, relationships, routines and every other priority in your life, swarm your mind all the time. Your doctor's appointments, grocery shopping list, mom's birthday, that big idea you had in the shower, bills you need to pay, systems you're trying to develop, text you forgot to respond to, and wait, did you leave the stove on this morning?! This scattered information hijacks your brain, leaving you overwhelmed or even worse...paralyzed.

There's something very cathartic about getting down all your thoughts. It sheds an instant clarity to what's most pressing and helps you process your emotions and feelings.

Stop thinking you'll remember

Every now and then something falls through the cracks, doesn't it?

Sometimes it's non-consequential, like forgetting to pick up batteries while you were at the store.

Sometimes it's embarrassing, like showing up to an event without your tickets.

Sometimes it makes you look really bad, like bringing one copy of a presentation to a meeting instead of three like your supervisor asked you to bring.

No matter what, it's frustrating when you forget to do, add, make, buy, dispose of, attach, create, or simply think about something you knew you were supposed to do.

For the love of all things empowering, please stop relying on your memory.

You put a lot of pressure on that extraordinary gift. It's already performing miracle after miracle, like lifting your arms, providing sensitivity to a hot stove, putting letters and sentence structures together so you can read this book, allowing you to mouth every word of "Material Girl" even though you haven't heard it in fifteen years. It is remarkable what our brains and memory can do. So why do we insist on stuffing it to overcapacity?

Important Note: When we're always relying on memory, we encounter brain fog, scatteredness, overwhelm, and anxiety. *Just sayin'.*

Instead, get as much out of your head and on paper as possible. (By paper I'm referring to a physical OR a digital source). Get into the habit of releasing all your thoughts so you leave room in your brain for fun thinking, strategy, or planning, like: What would be the best vacation this year? What are my most effective marketing tools? What do I need to do tonight, so I'm prepared for my appointment tomorrow morning?

Leave space for exploration, strategy, planning, and creativity, rather than mundane thoughts that you could easily capture on paper.

Your inability to keep everything straight, top-of-mind and in order also has a diminishing effect on your productivity. That's why it's critical to continuously **empty your brain.**

That means keeping a notepad with you (or a note-taking app on your phone) at all times. I prefer a digital list making app like Evernote or OneNote because chances are you have your phone with you everywhere, so you can always capture your thoughts, and you can use your lists All. The. Time.

I see many people using lists, perhaps some of the time or a lot of the time, but not all of the time. That's why a detail, step, or thought will fall through the cracks.

How many times have you remembered you needed to buy toothpaste just as you entered your garage, after going to the grocery store?

How about when you forgot to email that one document which ended up being the only one your boss or client asked about?

Getting into the habit of writing down all your thoughts, to-do's, tasks, and ideas create a safety net for your life. You never forget and you never waste time remembering what needs to be done.

Remember that cell phone battery analogy way back in Chapter One? Your brain is like your phone battery, where the more you use it, the faster your fully charged battery will go from green to red.

It's the same principle with keeping information stored in your head. The more information you keep up there, the more brain space you use every time you need to extract a piece of information.

For example, packing for a trip. About twenty times before, during, and after packing, you rummage through your mental checklist, for your pj's, underwear, toothbrush, directions, vitamins, itinerary, work shoes, gym shoes, party shoes, etc.

Which means each time you need to grab "hairbrush" or "earrings" from your memory, you're using up a vital piece of brain energy. (*Which means you get closer to hitting red on your battery bar*). You invest energy in remembering, double checking, and thinking about what you might have inadvertently forgotten. Not to mention the time and energy you'll spend on getting distracted each time you run from bathroom to bedroom to closet.

This is why I am obsessed with this simple, most overlooked, tool. It is THE way I keep my brain and life organized.

You and I both know that on top of that packing project our minds are drenched with a bajillion thoughts around work-related projects like proposals, financials, and projections. Our minds are constantly drawn towards thoughts of gifts to buy, reservations to make, meals to plan, linens to clean, decorations to put up, and packages to return.

Which is precisely why my obsession is particularly kick ass in high-stress periods of my life because it brings my anxiety down tenfold.

Before the "big reveal" it's important you keep an open mind and embrace the simplicity of this strategy, even if you're already doing it, and if you are, there's a good chance it could use a bit of improvement.

Here's what saves me miles of stress, hours of time, and buckets of energy.

Checklists.

Are you let down? Don't be. Given that something this simple could have a powerful effect on your life, you should be jumping for joy right now.

Why checklists?

Checklists get things out of your head. Which results in three very important benefits for your time and sanity:

- You free up mental space by not having to store all those tasks, next steps, chores, and to-do's in that precious brain of yours

- You save massive time in not having to think and re-think and remember, forget, and re-remember all "the things"

- You plummet your anxiety by avoiding thoughts like, "What was I supposed to do?" "Did I already do that?" "What's the other thing that had to get done?" etc.

Checklists also empower you with action steps. When created properly, they outline step-by-step, each consecutive task, so there is no need to think about what to do next.

Finally, checklists are satisfying. How many times have you completed a task that wasn't on your to-do list, then added it in just so you could cross it off? I'm onto you sweet stuff.

That dopamine shot (reward hormone) sets in, giving you a dose of instant gratification and the desire for more, more, more. Which simply means that the act of checking or crossing off gives you a sense of accomplishment and motivates you to keep going.

Plus, checklists give you clarity. When you're planning your day or even your morning, it's hard to figure out everything you need to get done, but when it's written down you can see your next steps, which drastically simplifies the planning process and inspires you to take action.

If you've committed to a digital tool, be sure it's downloaded and synced to your phone and other devices, so you have access to it on your phone, laptop, iPad, and any other device that's out there when you're reading this. Then, start recording *everything.*

Like if you don't want to forget that you need to start writing everything down, make that the first thing you write down. Every time you think of an idea, remember a task, or make a connection, simply – write it down. Having the comfort of knowing your thoughts won't be lost or forgotten, frees your mind to dream, brainstorm, and create.

With more room in your brain and less anxiety in your body, your productivity levels soar.

Although "emptying your brain" is a simple concept, it's not so simple to make it a habit. So, if capturing your thoughts all throughout the day seems daunting, here's how to get started:

Do a brain dump every night. Take 10 minutes to record every thought from over the course of the day, before you go to bed.

As you start to see and feel the benefits (which will happen almost immediately), you'll be inclined to start making it a habit throughout the day. On the other hand, when you skip your brain dump and your anxiety or overwhelm rises, you'll be inclined to pick up the habit again tomorrow. *Trust me on this one.*

This simple habit has been a life changer for me. Instead of having to reach waaay back into my mind to remember an idea, next step, or to-do, I tap my phone, get to my list, and happily exhale.

Remember, sometimes it's the tiniest changes in our lives that give us the biggest impact. Don't underestimate the power of a tweak.

When you wake up feeling overwhelmed

Sink full of dishes.

Nothing to wear.

Packed schedule.

Empty fridge.

Email overload.

Clutter everywhere.

Misplaced directions.

...and you haven't even had your coffee yet...

Feel familiar?

What do you do on those days when you wake up and everything feels overwhelming?

With so much to do, so little time and nothing going your way, it feels like the weight of the world is on your shoulders. It's the worst. Here are a few scenarios that I've played out in my past.

Wallow in self-pity.

Curse the world for my miserable life.

Pile blame upon blame of why things are like this.

Scream.

Shut down.

Not surprisingly, none of them helped the situation.

Feeling overwhelmed happens to everyone. No matter how well you plan your day or make or your lists, stress sneaks up on us. While you're in the experience, you might beat yourself up and think "How did I get here?"

Instead, ask yourself this: "What can I do to get myself out of feeling this way?"

Over years of practice here are three simple steps I've learned to take back control of my emotions and my day. I hope these few steps will inspire you to step back, release the weight of the world, and take action on what's truly valuable to you.

Step #1: Acknowledge the overwhelm

Yup, that's right. Take it in. Let it settle. Acknowledge what's happening.

Limit this time to 5 minutes. *Yes, five minutes.*

Not three hours of wallowing. Not two days of procrastinating.

Only 5 minutes to recognize you got a lot of shizzle going on and you need a plan to get out from under it.

Step #2: Make a comprehensive list (aka: Do the brain dump!)

Pull out a notepad and write, write, write, or jump on your list app and type, type, type. Get down everything swirling around in your brain. Like, things you need to get done, tasks to be completed, details you don't want to miss, appointments you can't forget, and projects that are on your mind.

This massive brain dump is cathartic. All those thoughts and ideas are mayhem in your brain. When you release them and see them visually, you'll immediately release the tension of forgetting something.

Writing your goals also brings clarity and focus. It gives you a direction. It's a powerful reminder that you can use to keep yourself on the right track when you feel stressed (especially at times like this).

You'll better connect the dots of where and how you can make things happen. You'll get clarity on what's on your plate, what's truly urgent, and what can be put off until tomorrow or later.

Step #3: Take the next most important action

Look at your list ask yourself this: "What are the THREE THINGS that are going to make the biggest difference in my life right now?"

Maybe it's not the dishes or the laundry or the bills or the other hundred things that are in plain sight, making you cuh-razy. Perhaps it's getting the directions, calling the doctor, or paying your vendor bill.

Then based on your answer to this question: "What is the next best action I could take right now?"

Then do it. Just. Like. That. Go to your closet, print out the map, or speed dial your OB. No overthinking. No overcomplicating. No fretting about when or how everything else will get done.

Just focus on that ONE NEXT RIGHT step and do it. You will immediately feel better.

When you're done, rinse and repeat. Look at your list and take action on the second-best item you could tackle next. Rinse and repeat.

Then the third. Rinse and repeat.

Here's a question I constantly ask myself:

"If there were only three things I could get done all day, what would they be?" Of course, there are about

87,000 other things you'd like to get done in a day, but what are your TOP THREE? What are the MOST IMPORTANT tasks that you really have to get done?

Focus on those and watch your motivation and productivity take on new heights. Okay, so those are the steps I go through when I'm drowning in overwhelm, and I know you can do these too.

Quick Recap:

1) Acknowledge the overwhelm, but don't wallow more than 5 minutes!

2) Do a massive brain dump (write it ALL down)!

3) Prioritize and focus on your TOP 3 most important tasks.

Finally, breathe and have faith that everything will be okay. You've survived the rocky waters before, and you'll do it again. Have faith in yourself, in your strength, and in your ability to survive and thrive. Know that you will come out stronger on the other side.

When you're deep in that exasperating moment of total overwhelm, close your eyes, take a deep breath and compose yourself. Remind yourself you've been here before and you're still here. Today, this time, you will cope even better. You'll do your brain dump, you'll take action on a task, and you WILL be okay.

Writing the perfect to do list

Ok, so you've brain dumped. You've gotten it all out. Now what? You're looking at fourteen pages of to-do's, thinking you were so much better off pretending you had nothing going on in your life.

You take one glance at that list and get a visceral reaction to that long and daunting inventory of everything you still need to get done. I can relate. Especially at 2:36 a.m. when I'm lying in overwhelm, my mind swirling with everything lurking over me. This doesn't happen to me much anymore because understanding one simple concept literally changed my life.

The *way* I wrote my to-do lists.

Here's what a typical list used to look like:

- ☐ Website

- ☐ Financials

- ☐ Vacation plans

- ☐ Sales funnel

When I was in the midst of my already hectic schedule, I'd look at that list and want to throw-up *or begin drinking*. Neither of which were particularly helpful in getting through my day.

Here's how I would typically get through the list in my mind.

Website. I need to update my testimonials, create landing pages, and change all my images. Who would give me feedback? What software should I use for my opt-in? Should I hire a photographer? Ok, waaaay too much to think about right now. Let's move onto the next item.

Financials. The word itself gives me a panic attack. I hate spreadsheets. Don't even know where to begin. Getting knots in my stomach. Next!

Vacation Plans. Which beach should we go to? Should I look into flights? Do we have miles? Maybe we should drive? Too many questions. I need to move on. Next!

It would continue like this as I'd make my way down the list. Without clear direction, I'd go around in circles, barely making headway.

It took me a long time to discover that website, financials, and vacation plans are NOT to-dos. They are NOT action items. Those are all PROJECTS made up of many action items. And making this shift in the way I wrote my lists, was the ah-ha moment that changed my life.

There are two key steps to make your lists work effectively:

#1: Break down all your projects into detailed tasks
#2: Use a verb (an action) in each of your tasks

Using that formula, here's what "Website" on my list might look like now.

Website Project

- ☐ *Create* testimonial form on Google Docs

- ☐ *Email* form to Sandy, Jim, and Ron

- ☐ *Upload* response to testimonial page on site

- ☐ *Call* photographer to schedule session date

- ☐ *Pick out* outfit for photoshoot

- ☐ *Create* list of different shots to review with photographer

Each small, specific step is outlined, starting with a verb (an action) so I know exactly what needs to get done.

Which means instead of four tasks on my list, I may end up with forty. This might make you think, "Isn't forty more overwhelming than four?"

Actually, it's not, because the detailed task-based list, although longer, is CLEAR and ACTIONABLE. Unlike the "project-based lists" it gives you direction and motivates immediate action. "Website" gives you no direction on what to do, but "Create testimonial form on Google Docs" tells you exactly what needs to be done next.

Now, instead of feeling overwhelmed and panicked when I look at my list, I start moving forward on projects. (**Hint:** small detailed tasks help you avoid procrastination).

Chances are when you see "organize garage" on your list you'll find 1,800 reasons why you never have the time or resources to get it done. If you see "take old bikes to Goodwill" on your list, chances are you'll figure out a time and way to get it done. When you find yourself procrastinating on a project, break it down into super small tasks and focus on just one task at time.

If you find that you have too many tasks under a Project and it's just overwhelming, break them down further into sub-projects so they're more doable and motivate you to take action.

For example, if you have a full page of tasks under "Vacations," break it up into mini-projects under "Vacations" like:

- Spring break

- Summer beach trip

- NY wedding weekend

Here's what a revised, more actionable list will look like.

VACATIONS (Project)

- ☐ **Spring Break** (Sub-Project)
    - ☐ Confirm hotel reservations (task)
    - ☐ Buy camera lens (task)
    - ☐ Take photos of passports (task)
    - ☐ Print out packing list (task)
- ☐ **Summer Beach Trip** (Sub-Project)
    - ☐ Buy new towels (task)
    - ☐ Book Sunday brunch place (task)
    - ☐ Confirm dog sitter (task)
    - ☐ Send deposit (task)
- ☐ **NY Wedding Weekend** (Sub-Project)
    - ☐ Send RSVP (task)
    - ☐ Buy plane ticket (task)
    - ☐ Book hotel room (task)
    - ☐ Buy wedding gift from registry (task)

Actionable smaller tasks within each sub-project will help you prioritize, move forward, plan, and even delegate tasks to other people.

If you do this one step, I promise you will feel more in control of your time and day. You will have everything you need to start operating from a place of clarity and planning, rather than confusion and uncertainty.

So, my composed and organized friend, once you get your awesomely organized and action-taking lists together, where do you store them?

I'm not gonna lie. I loves me some paper. I could spend hours in a stationary store surrounded by journals with sticker sheets, pocket folders, and inspirational quotes, oohing and aahing over leather-bound planners, embossed notebooks, and ribbon bookmarks with gorgeous floral motifs.

Alas, experience has shown me that too many times I haven't gotten my moment-to-moment thoughts and to-do's out of my head because my notebook or planner wasn't with me. It was in the car, on my desk, forgotten on the washer, or really, who knows where – exactly as I've needed it most.

Since thoughts come to us all the time, I recommend moving from a paper planner to using a digital resource to capture them, like *Evernote* or *OneNote*.

If the thought of giving up your precious paper is giving you a minor heart attack, stay calm and read on.

I personally made the move from my beloved paper planners to the online world, always having access to my lists on my phone, laptop, and iPad. Without a doubt, I attribute it to reaching all new levels of productivity, efficiency, and ease, and there is no there is no way I am going back.

Keeping your lists organized on Evernote or OneNote makes it easier to:

- Add and delete rows (Every single day, more like, every single hour, you will be adding to, and subtracting from lists and it's hard to squeeze in rows on paper).

- Share your lists (with colleagues, family, or volunteer group)

- Keep it at your fingertips at all time (you'll have access to it on all your devices)

- Keep everything in one place (Buh-bye random sticky notes and backs of envelopes)

- Eliminate the fear of losing or destroying notebooks (what if coffee spills on it or you leave it at the grocery store?)

- See everything you have going on in one complete view (toggle back and forth between daily, weekly, and monthly views)

- Make decisions on how to prioritize and where to spend your time

Once you start using this system and have the confidence that all your thoughts and ideas are stored in one accessible place, you will really begin to appreciate this system. No more wasting time on trying to remember if and where you wrote something down or saved information.

Key to making this work: Always keep your Evernote or OneNote tab open on your computer. Whenever a thought comes to your mind or you want to capture information add it in.

Hopefully, you see the value of using one easy-to-access place for your lists as true sanity savers, and you see the benefits of adopting the habit of getting everything out of your head, All. The. Time. Not just when it's convenient or when you feel like it or when you're overwhelmed. (Although those are three great times to do it too). Make it a part of your routine, a natural part of your lifestyle, an innate response.

Let's recap why it's so important:

- You will think more clearly and at higher levels

- You will feel an increase in productivity and creativity when you're not burning all that energy on pulling information from all different parts of your brain

- You will sleep better. No more waking up at 3:30 a.m. with thoughts of "did I remember to send that email?!"

- You will be more present. Look forward to better listening skills, conversations, and relationships

- You will lose the fear of tasks falling through the cracks or duplicating efforts

- You will get more of the right things done

Awesome ideas can pop up at the strangest times, but they tend to not stay for long in your head. So, you need to capture them fast or they are gone in a flash.

When you don't occupy your mind with having to remember every little thing – like you need to stop for toilet paper on the way home – you become less stressed and it becomes easier to think clearly. Feeling calmer not only improves your health but also makes life easier and more and more rewarding.

Gone are the days where we can remember everything we need to know and do. We constantly need to be on top of things, usually an extraordinary amount of things, which makes it easy to feel overwhelmed or get bogged down in information overload.

The issue is that while information, tasks, distractions, and responsibilities keep piling up, the space in our brains and the number of hours we have stay the same.

Writing things down is a simple yet powerful way to record anything and everything that has your attention — your client meetings, home renovation list, that killer idea you had on your drive, your brother-in-law's birthday, the habits you're trying to develop, that quote you loved, that song you heard and can't wait to download. It's life changing when you have access to them any time you want.

Lastly, I want to leave you with this: **Writing things down helps keep you motivated.**

No matter who you are or what you've accomplished, motivation dwindles over time. Even when you start off totally pumped and energetic you eventually find yourself losing momentum or getting sucked back into the rabbit hole of distractions or self-doubt.

Writing things down, especially your top and most relevant goals for the day reminds you of your purpose on a regular basis. I've mentioned before that I can use all the reinforcements I can get when it comes to staying on task and keeping motivated. Whether you have them listed in your phone, on a sticky note stuck to your fridge, or an index card taped to your mirror, it's best to keep your goals visible as a constant reminder.

Don't be afraid or embarrassed or shy to pull out your phone right in the middle of a conversation when your hubby asks you to pick up three packs of triple-A batteries, but not the ones with the Coppertop, while your daughter is clawing at your jeans because there are no Pop Tarts left. Smack in the midst of your talk and/or whiny request, pull out your list and type the things you don't want to forget.

Instead of looking like someone who can't remember anything (so she needs to write it down), you will look like someone totally in control. A lady with a system. On top of her shizzle.

Embrace this life-changing strategy. You will feel so much more confident knowing that nothing will be forgotten or fall through the cracks. Which makes for a more relaxing day, a more patient human being, and a perfect opportunity to feel more accomplished.

Mules (Mridu's Rules) For Being Less Scattered
Don't move on to the next Chapter before going through the next short exercise:

1. Take 15-20 minutes to empty out of your brain. Get every thought, to-do, and task out of your head!

2. Put on your timer for 20 minutes to re-organize your list into projects, sub-projects, and tasks.

(Join me at www.lifeisorganized.com/rightthings for a free resource for all the exercises).

Chapter Seven:
Get Out of Chaos

(Code Letter: "S")

Growing up I spent most of my summers in India. My parents emigrated to the U.S. right after I was born, so much of my close family were still there, in their home cities of Mumbai (formerly Bombay) and New Delhi. India is more than another country. It is truly another world. A juxtaposition of traditional and modern life, it's colorful, bleary, loud, polluted, extremely impoverished, and exceedingly wealthy.

I'd leave my American world and be transported to my Indian world the moment I'd step foot on the overstuffed Pan Am 747. As soon as the plane doors opened in Delhi, the pungent smell of cooking fires, incense, sweat, and heat would overtake our senses. I was always amazed how the airport and streets would be bustling even at our 2:00 a.m. arrival.

From the comforts of our steaming hot showers and air-conditioned homes, we'd shift to heating bath water with a geyser, filled up in a bucket to pour on our bodies, cups by cup, and daily power outages in the 120-degree heat.

At night time, I would lay in bed uncomfortably until I couldn't hold my pee in any longer and tiptoe my way to the bathroom, in fear that a stealthy lizard patrolling the walls and ceilings would spot an American and jump on my neck for a closer look.

Every moment of every day in India is sensory overload, from the masses of people gushing from all directions to the malnourished cows and stray dogs meandering through the roads. There is one thing that stands out more than anything, and I've heard this from countless friends, tourists, and family that visit The Motherland. It's the traffic. *It. Is. Like. Nothing. Else.*

Imagine endless rivers of cars intersecting in every way possible. Now, times that by ten. Now, throw in bicycles, three-wheelers, carts, scooters, and hordes of people and you'll probably still be underestimating the level of chaos by about...hmmm...80 percent.

When I took my kids to India ten years ago, even they, as four and seven-year olds, were in awe of what was happening. "Where are the traffic lights, mommy?" "Why does everyone use their horn so much?" "This is weird."

To us foreigners used to our massive grid systems and coordinated traffic light matrices, there appears to be no system at all, but in reality, in India, everyone gets where they need to be, even amidst the chaos.

The truth is, we *all* have some level of chaos in our lives, and we, too, get to our destination at some point. Whether it's work, a promotion, school, vacations...we'll figure out a way to make it happen. To get by. To get to the places we need to go. Does it need to be under such nerve-racking, overwhelming, and painfully slow circumstances? Wouldn't it be fun to enjoy a less turbulent ride?

We spend so much of our lives in chaos and confusion. Figuring it out while we go along, flying by the seat of our pants. Whether it's stressing over what to make for dinner at 5 o'clock or deciding what to wear when you're already running late, to evaluating how to analyze monthly projections when you have a hundred other things going on.

Yes, I get that you *can* live that way. That ultimately, you will figure how to get a meal in your belly or your kids to school, but without a good system, is it worth all the added stress and overwhelm?

I think not.

Stress adds up in your life big time. It affects your body, thoughts, relationships, clarity, feelings, and behavior. It contributes to weight gain, sleepless nights, low performance, and generally cranky conversations. It can contribute to health problems, anxiety, depression, feeling overwhelmed, and a lack of motivation and focus.

Now that I've brought this conversation to a low point, let's talk about how to uplift yourself out of anxiety and into that serene well-oiled machine you've always wondered how "other people" have.

If I had to choose one determinant to bolster ANY results, it would beee… *Drumroll please…*

…Strengthening systems and processes.

Not the sexy and glamorous pill you were hoping for? Don't worry. I'm going to show you how. By focusing on process improvement, all your other goals will be achieved.

You probably have some lofty goals in your life. Move to the next level. Get healthier. Stop binge-watching TV. Spend more time with your family, or, perhaps you've committed to hitting a certain revenue number, growing your team, or expanding your services.

Any of those goals will accelerate with a system in place.

Take sales for example. If your goal is to increase sales by 50% by raising your prices as well as the volume you sell, you might provide your team with numbers to hit every week or month

The system *behind* those numbers is where the magic happens, such as:

- What is the exact script or conversation with a new prospect?

- What information should be captured?

- What should be offered to convert that prospect to a lead?

- When should you upsell or down sell a prospect?

- What letterhead should be used?

None of those answers are left to chance or experience when a system is in place.

There are endless opportunities to create processes and systems in your work or business. Any time you are doing something that can be done the same way, over and over, you have a chance to make it as efficient as possible.

You may have a system for:

- An invoice to go out when a certain part of a project is complete

- The way you prepare for a sales presentation

- A specific way you add flour to your famous cupcakes that customers rave about

- An email sequence that nurtures the people who subscribe to your mailing list

- Your social media posts by weekly and daily themes

There are also endless opportunities to create processes and systems in your home and personal life because let's face it, if you can't get out of the door on time or get home without panicking about having clean underwear for tomorrow, you work day isn't going to start off that great.

You may have a system for:

- Planning your groceries and meals
- Cleaning your home
- Doing your laundry
- Getting bills done
- Home maintenance
- Picking out outfits every day

If you're worried that systemizing will make you rigid or deny you of creativity in any way, you are mistaken, my friend. Systems invite freedom.

They provide massive results by:

- Freeing up your time and allowing you to automate
- Delegating while still maintaining appropriate control
- Inviting creativity. If all you are doing is working IN your business, how are you ever going to find time to work ON your business?
- Delivering a consistent and excellent experience
- Lowering costs. You don't waste time and effort reinventing the wheel each time you're going through a process

- Minimizing the fear that something may fall through the cracks

- Making it easier to train others

It's no surprise that the more I've systemized every part of my business, the more revenue I've generated and the less overwhelmed I've felt. The icing on the cake is that systems have allowed better tracking and analysis than ever before, which has impacted where I spend my three most important resources: time, energy, and money.

For example, by documenting a consistent referral system I now have data on the number of clients I'm communicating with, where the best referrals are coming from, and what industries yield the highest revenue.

Let me be transparent here. I am a far cry from a data analyst and would never be considered a "numbers person." My system was created on a Google doc and didn't require a fancy or complicated software. *I'm all about easy-peasy.*

This system provided me with information to invest marketing dollars more effectively this year, which made me and my accountant very happy.

I recently helped a client feel less stressed, scattered, and unfocused by systemizing her social media efforts. We picked daily themes, created a repository of images and quotes, and scheduled all her posts. She tripled her engagement with her audience in the last couple weeks while halving the time she spent on it. Not to mention she's ready to delegate this task to someone else on her team.

Another client of mine wanted to lose 15 pounds. (She'd been trying to hit this goal for three years on and off). She'd tried eating healthier and working out when she could, but without a real system in place, her efforts were inconsistent and haphazard.

With a process for meal planning, grocery delivery, workout schedule (which meant rejiggering work schedules) and daily check-ins, she hit her goal in less than a quarter.

Systems are liberating. They give you the freedom of time, space, energy, serenity, and money.

Ok, so hopefully you're clear and excited about the why, but you might be wondering, "...and how exactly do I get this system in place?" Lucky for you, I love simple three-step processes, so let's go through it now.

Step #1: Identify the types of actions you take regularly to drive your business or make your home life more efficient.

Signs for creating new systems are:

- Repetitive Tasks: What same or similar tasks are you doing frequently? Examples: Answering the same questions over and over again, creating a weekly or monthly newsletter, making meals, cleaning the house, and doing laundry.

- <u>Frustrating and/or Overwhelming Process:</u> What experiences (that are in your control) frustrate you over the course of the day? Example: Getting out of the house in the morning, invoicing and billing clients, setting up appointments.

- <u>Inconsistent Results:</u> Do you or your team have inconsistent results from frequent tasks? Example: Walking out of a meeting with different information each time or team members reporting on varying stats.

- <u>Successful Methodology:</u> What can you replicate from an experience that has run smoothly? Example: Bring extra copies of your documents, grab specific notebooks, keep a charger in the car, get directions the night before.

List 5 areas you will benefit from creating a new or improved system or process at your work and 5 other areas you will benefit from creating one at home. Of the areas you listed, what new system will have the greatest impact on your business and/or your home life?

Step #2: Create documentation for your #1 system identified above.

Every system or process must be documented! That means it needs to get out of your head and down on paper (or more likely, in a digital format). Remember, keeping all the information in your brain leads to information overload, not to mention confusion and loss of clarity. Documentation should be very detailed, broken down in easy, step-by-step directions.

What are the steps from beginning to end for your process, including all the little baby steps? The ones you want to overlook or like to assume someone else will understand when they're reading your document, even though you haven't specified it.

Think of your step-by-step directions like a Lego manual. You know how a five-year old or a ninety-five-year-old can pick up a Lego manual and thirty minutes later end up with a sports car?

That is how you want to think about the directions you're creating. Do not assume that other people understand what is in your head or that seems obvious to you. Anyone should be able to pick up the document, follow step-by-step directions, and successfully complete it.

Here are a few simple ways to help make that happen.

- Use concise bulleted and numbered formats (drop the long sentences and paragraphs)

- Use photos along the way (again think Legos)

- Leave white space between steps

- Breakdown steps into different phases.

    o For example:

        ▪ Phase One: Set-Up

- Phase Two: Build

- Phase Three: Double Check Steps

Your new process can be created on a Google sheet or doc, Evernote, or in a project management tool like Asana or Trello. You can also create them in forms of my most beloved, checklists. (For a review on the beauty of this simple but powerful tool, check out Chapter 6 again). Here's the quick refresher, plus an example of how you can use them to create foolproof systems.

Create checklists so no steps are missed or duplicated. All team members (or family members) including yourself, will know where you are in a process at all times. Below is an example of the start of a checklist I use for creating my weekly blogs. When I was finally ready to delegate this task, I needed a simple way to ensure my assistant would have a consistent experience every week and not miss or duplicate any steps.

In my head, I thought there were about 20-25 steps to get my blog up and ready to publish. Then, when I actually broke down each step into detail, like what font colors to use, what titles to save, images, and how to include SEO keywords, there were over 60 steps! Sixty steps. That's a lot of unnecessary room being taken up in my head.

Even though I had gone through the process hundreds of times, I often had a nagging feeling that I was forgetting a step or would wake up at 3:00 a.m.

thinking, "Did I add a border to yesterday's photo?" With a simple checklist, all of that worry and second-guessing disappeared, and my energy soared during this process. Rather than expending energy pulling from my memory, I simply opened my list and worked my way down. *Easy-peasy.*

Before jumping into next steps, let me reiterate how freeing it is to grab a list. *Yes, when I know of a good thing, I like to beat people over the head with it.* You will save loads of time and energy when your process is out of your head, when it is in an easy format to read, and when it is super clear. Bonus! Having documented processes will help you stop procrastinating. *Say whaaatt??*

Yes, you heard me.

Picture this: You've booked a new client. You're ecstatic and can't wait to get started with them. Once you come down from cloud nine you have to deal with the administrative side of things, which isn't quite as exciting. Get an agreement in place, create invoices, set them up in your client system, input your notes and their personal information, send them a welcome packet, etc. So many things to do on top of your 93 other tasks on your to-do list, you put it off for later, or tomorrow, or the next day. Until you're under the gun, wondering if you sent them everything you needed to.

Welcome to scenario two. You've booked a new client, have come down from cloud nine, and need to deal with the administrative side of things. With one click, you open up your "New Client Onboarding" checklist.

It looks something like this:

Calls

- [ ] Set up recurring coaching call
- [ ] Check on holidays etc.
- [ ] Add client cell number to phone

Agreement

- [ ] Update agreement: change names in FOUR places and DATES
- [ ] Download signed agreement
- [ ] Send reminder to sign

Email

- [ ] Send "here's what to expect next" email
- [ ] Request mailing address and birthday

Invoicing

- [ ] Create invoice

Shared Folder

- [ ] Create shared folder
- [ ] Add signed document in shared folder
- [ ] Verify they can get in before our call

Files To Update

- [ ] update "Client Roster" file
- [ ] update "Client Schedule" file
- [ ] Add signed document in Google Drive folder
- [ ] Send text or email to get address and birthday
- [ ] Create reminders for accountability

You set a 25-minute timer (use the FocusKeeper app) and work your way down the list without freaking out, thinking about what to do next, or worrying you forgot something. You save loads of energy and thinking-power by relying on your list instead of your brain. With this added level of ease, simplicity, and efficiency, your procrastination reflexes take a sharp turn and instead guide towards thoughts like, "this is easy to knock out."

That, my sweet friend, is the power of a system... of a list... of a process. It takes you beyond "here's a plan" to realms of "I know how to easily get it done."

The opportunities for checklists (aka step-by-step systems) are truly endless. Try on a travel checklist, meal planning checklist, bills to pay checklist, evening routine checklist, morning routine checklist, packing up for school checklist, personal hygiene checklist (if you have two boys, you'll understand this one). It goes on and on and on.

The more you get into the habit of creating systems for every little part of your home, business, or life, the easier they will run, and the more consistent results will be.

For you visual folks

A system or process can also be represented in a visual drawing, also known as flowcharts.

Here's a quick 4-step one:

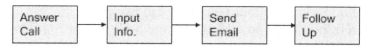

1. Answer Call

2. Input Prospect Information in CRM System

3. Send Introduction Email

4. Follow Up in Two Days To Confirm Receipt of Info.

Here are considerations to think about:

- At what points are decisions made?

- Where have breakdowns occurred in the past?

- Have you captured all the information you need?

- Is every contact/touchpoint in your workflow?

Charts are also a very effective way to visually see your steps, systems or processes, and they're not just for kids! Some of my most successful clients use visual charts, both with their businesses and families, to keep everyone on track, know their responsibilities, and keep things from falling through the cracks.

Typically, you might think about chore charts or cleaning charts (which are brilliant) but don't dismiss charts for personal or professional goals too. You might have a chart for daily sales activities, like making two calls, sending three follow-up emails, and reaching out to one new contact.

I don't know about you, but I can use every reinforcement possible to get me to do things I like to put off. A task on my calendar usually isn't enough. It's more like a scheduled task, a reminder, a sticky note, a chart, and then maybe, just maybe, I'll stay on the right track.

These tools are simple and powerful. So, don't take them from granted or ignore them. Also, don't spend hours and hours on creating them. Those perfectionist tendencies are just covers disguised as procrastination techniques.

I know your type because I'm one of them. I've spent countless hours and days on creating the perfect color-coded hourly chart, dissecting and highlighting my personal care time from my family time to my work time to my friend's time to my spiritual time. That was a lot of time spent on a routine I didn't even follow.

This is precisely why I've moved over to simple spreadsheets and Google Docs. No more fancy-schmancy scrapbooked poster board for me. Look, if that's what lights you up, go for it, but give yourself a time limit. Like one hour, not one week.

You can always tweak, enhance, and prettify your charts, checklists, and systems down the road, but for now, **done is better than perfect.** Don't let perfectionism get in the way of reaching your goals, making your life easier, and feeling awesome at the end of each day.

I can't tell you how challenging this has been for me writing this book. I've been told over and over again to write. Just write. Don't edit along the way. Finish a first draft and then go back and do it at the end. That. Is. Hard. The perfectionist in me wants to rewrite every run-on sentence and carefully craft each paragraph with a beginning, middle, and end. You know where I'd be right now if I were using that strategy? Back in Chapter Two. I know I'll have time to edit later, to perfect, to rewrite, and to reorganize, but for now, I've just got to get the right things done.

Don't recreate the wheel

When I was eight or nine years old, I got a Fashion Angels design sketch set for Christmas, which was right up there with my battery-operated Holly Hobbie sewing machine, and my to die for Lite Brite set.

I was psyched. Already always walking around with a pad and pencil in my hand or in my Smurfs backpack. I couldn't wait to take my drawing skills to the next level. I could design stunning fashions for the Fashion Angels models, use the stencils to trace clothing and accessories, and shade details with color crayons. There was even a glittery crayon which pretty much knocked me out of the universe.

I would spend hours carefully sketching the models before even getting to the design, stencils, and stickers. To my surprise, I was not as gifted as I thought I was. My sketches didn't remotely resemble those of the runway models on the set cover.

One day my dad saw me struggling to create the outline and he suggested I take the one they'd included in the box and trace it over and over, so I could spend my time on the fun stuff, like adding enormous shoulder pads and gaudy rhinestone jewelry.

"Wouldn't that be cheating?"

"It's not cheating. It's smart. You can focus on the parts you like to do."

Hmmm…He made a good point. Instead of spending an hour on that same base of the Fashion Angel, I could trace ten copies and spend hours on lavender and pink rainbow and cloud patterns on their t-shirts and legwarmers. Brilliant!

I'm betting you have a ton of opportunities to systemize information, processes, or foundations in your life right now. In the adult world, we call these templates.

Templates are great for emails, questions, or information you are repeatedly creating/answering. Like, how about those five or six questions you get asked about regarding your return policy, sign up process, or location, over and over again? What about the contract you have to send out every time you get a new client?

Don't waste your time constantly recreating the wheel. Keep a document of templates so you're not wasting time recreating similar information. Create templates for this information in forms of an FAQ page on your website or a Commonly Asked Questions sheet you can easily email.

Email templates are one of my favorite ways to save time, respond quickly, and avoid procrastinating to write them. I have templates for when I'm introducing myself to someone new, reaching out for a speaking engagement, thanking someone after a conversation, following up about an order, providing next steps for coaching, training requirements, and many more.

The great thing about a template is that it includes the base information but allows you to customize and personalize each email or communication when necessary. Add in a personal note, change their name, refer to a conversation you had, and update next steps. All that is a lot easier and less dreadful when you're working with a foundation already in place.

I save these emails in my Gmail folder under a label called "Templates." Then each email is saved and labeled accordingly like, "Speaking Follow-Up Template" or "Great to Meet You Template." When I'm ready to craft my email, I simply go to the email, copy, paste, and customize.

I not only feel so accomplished by whizzing through my responses and follow ups in half the time, it gives me a sense of control and efficiency. Which is so much more empowering than flying by the seat of my pants or always feeling behind.

Before I wrap up this step of documenting your processes, I must include video again, as it's one of my favorite ways to get information out of my head and into a format that's easy to use and understand. Video tutorials are very effective for computer-based tasks and can be used as the guide itself or in addition to a guide.

Let's say you use a software once a month or every few months to update financials or customer information. After weeks of not using it, naturally, you forget which of the dozens of tabs and pulldowns to select. You remember it took you ten minutes to figure out where to put the cost estimate, but now you can't find it again. You waste twenty minutes each time you use the software just getting to the basic information.

Instead, hit record while the process is fresh on your mind, so you can watch a short tutorial the next time around. Videos of your screen can be taken on Zoom, Screenflow, or QuickTime (which is usually installed on most computers).

Step #3: Test, Analyze, Tweak

Now that you've identified where you could benefit from systems and you've documented one in a step-by-step way that makes it simple for anyone to pick up and go, you're ready to put it to test.

Put your system to use and in practice with yourself and with other team members. Test drive its effectiveness. Chances are you'll find areas for improvement where there is confusion or missing steps. This is a good thing. Each modification will get you closer to a successful system to use now and as your business/career grows.

Ask yourself and your team or family members:

- Does this feel simple and easy to understand or frustrating and difficult to use/navigate?

- Have I had a positive experience with this system?

- Am I using my resources wisely?

Tip #1: Don't get caught up in making it perfect, because systems evolve.

Rarely are you one and done. But with a great foundation, future updates are easy to implement.

Bottom line, I use systems a lot, and you should too.

- In my business, I coach, speak and train — all of which leverage the same knowledge, information, and expertise, so I'm not always recreating. I document processes for blog creation, speaking, invoicing, sales conversations, and many other parts of my business. I create and use templates for emails, follow-ups, sign up forms, etc. I have certain days and times set for clients every week.

- In my home, laundry, groceries, and errands are done on the weekend. Everyone in our family knows this and are aware of their responsibilities. The boys wash and dry their clothes. I fold. They put away on Sunday night. I use meal plans so I'm not struggling with dinner ideas at 5:00 p.m. *When I have off weeks and don't do this, I always regret it!*

With these routines in place, I'm not worried about when these tasks will get done. Which leaves me for more time to enjoy my kiddos, read my books, hang with my besties, volunteer, go to Zumba, love on my hubby, and drink my wine. In other words, to focus on the things that matter most.

Tip #2: Turbo-charge your systems

Want to skyrocket your systems to super efficiency level? *Spoiler alert: It's a divine place!*

Try Batching.

The idea of batching means to do a set of similar tasks at one time, rather than spreading smaller jobs over a number of days. It saves time in retrieving and putting away supplies and helps keep you focused on one task only. Batching will help you remain consistent with your organization.

At home, for example:

- Rather than vacuuming one room, then doing another room a separate day or time, vacuum the whole house in one go

- Rather than doing a few items of ironing every other day, wait until you have a big load of ironing to complete in one sitting

- Rather than doing your groceries over several times during the week, batch your food shopping and do it all on one day of the week

- Rather than prepping and cooking meals every night, batch your meal preparation on a Saturday or Sunday, so you have meals ready to go for the week

At work, for example:

- Rather than brainstorming and writing a new blog or newsletter every week, schedule one day to write four of them

- Rather than invoicing clients sporadically, do them all in one sitting at a set time every week

- Rather than create social media posts daily, get them done in one block of time and schedule them out over the month

- Rather than reacting to emails every two minutes, batch them in 30-minute chunks, three times over the day.

Grouping similar work into batches allows you to stay more focused, feel less scattered, and be more efficient with your time.

If I wasn't batching my work, my week would go something like this:

Monday

- Write a to-do list

- Work on a blog post

- Answer emails

- Run a coaching call

- Network on social media

- Post on Facebook

- Check emails

- Work on course creation

- Post on Instagram

- Answer more emails

Then all the following days of the week would be pretty similar. It would be exhausting and would probably take at least 30-35 hours/week.

Instead, my week goes more like this:

Monday

- Write four blog posts (6 hours)

- Email (1 hour))

Tuesday

- Film four videos (3 hours)

- Network on social media (30 minutes)

Wednesday

- Coaching calls (5 hours)

- Email (1 hour)

Thursday

- Course creation (4 hours)

Friday

- Course creation (3 hours)
- Networking (1 hour)

This is only about 23 hours per week.

Now, I'm not saying I couldn't find other things to do to fill up my 30 or 40-hour work week. I'm just showing you how efficient it could be to get the same amount of work done when you're focused and batching your activities and days vs. being scattered and doing it all, all the time.

One of my favorite things about taking this approach with my business is that it means that not only is nearly every day quite different, but each week is different as well.

As you saw in the above example, one week I might be focused on writing blog posts, filming videos, and course creation, but then the next week I might focus on finishing up the course. The week after that I might fill entirely with creating/managing ad campaigns and writing emails for my list. Each week, I can choose to focus on what I'm feeling the most interested in, but I know that my activities will be moving my business forward.

I also switch up my days to help my clients. One week I coach on Tuesdays and Thursdays, and the next week I coach on Mondays and Wednesdays.

This also allows my clients flexibility when they're choosing a day to work with me.

Keep in mind that batching will only work if you plan ahead. If you don't, then you won't be able to write four blog posts tomorrow, because you'll need to: answer emails, post on Facebook, update your website, call your clients, etc.

So, plan to batch (get your plan in place) of what you'll do each day next week. You'll be surprised at how much progress you can make with your business in way less time then you generally spend. Imagine how amazing it will feel to have all of your administrative tasks complete or blog posts written by end of day Monday!

The idea and benefits of batching (also known as "theming") are summed up well by John Dumas of EOFire:

"Every single week, on Sunday, I would find myself writing our email newsletter that was supposed to go out on Monday. Sometimes I'd start it on Wednesday or Thursday, but without fail, it was always on Sunday that I found myself finishing it.

Now that I have an entire writing day, I don't have to break it up like that anymore. Given an entire day to write, I'm able to account for anything I need to get done that week for writing like blog posts, campaign emails, and newsletters. Whereas before, I'd maybe write the blog on Tuesday, the email newsletter on Thursday and Sunday, and the campaign emails on Friday. Now that I have a writing day, all of these tasks are accomplished on Monday's – for the entire week – which prevents any type of writing "popping up" on my schedule throughout the week. Theming (or Batching) your days is going to help you be more efficient and get more done."

Systems rule. There's simply no greater truth. Systems are the structure around which the other parts of our work and life are framed and without them, we tolerate chaos.

I hope I've helped inspire you to implement some systems in your life where they don't exist or spruce up the ones you do. If you're serious about focusing on the things that matter most take a crack at implementing a new system using a checklist, chart, or document. Batch your like tasks. Batch your days for similar tasks.

Other people will follow your system when they understand the value it brings to your home or customer, the quality of your life and the results that you get, but most importantly, because they too, will come to believe that it's the simplest route to getting the right things accomplished.

Mules (Mridu's Rules) For Getting Out of Chaos
Don't move on to the next Chapter before going
through the next short exercise:

List 5 areas you will benefit from creating a new or
improved system or process.

_____

_____

_____

_____

_____

Of the areas you listed, what new system will have
the greatest impact on your business and/or life?

_____

_____

What tool will you use to put your new system into
place? (Ex. Checklist, Step-by-step document, video
tutorial, chart, batch tasks, batch days).

_____

_____

DO IT!!!!!!

(Come on over to
www.lifeisorganized.com/rightthings for a free
resource for all the exercises).

Chapter Eight:
Anything is Possible

I once knew a young girl who was quite certain of the saying "She'd lose her head if it wasn't attached to her," originated from her parents as they'd find themselves rehashing yet another story of how she misplaced her jacket, money, or keys.

Her mom would send her to school in real gold earrings (with secure backs) and yet she'd come home with only one, no idea the other was even missing. Her dad would give her lunch money, and she'd come home hungry, because somewhere between clapping Miss Mary Mack on the school bus and double Dutch jump roping on the playground, she'd lose it.

One evening, as a teenager, she went shopping with her mom and bought a new blazer, killer jeans, and a gorgeous top she was allowed to splurge on. When they got to their car, the girl realized her hands were empty. Her bag of awesomeness was somewhere in the mall. She retraced every store, dressing room, and pit stop they made. Asked every register attendant and scoured the Lost and Found, but no bag of just-paid-for, beautiful clothes to be found.

Her shame heightened when she had to explain to her father how she lost hundreds of dollars' worth of clothes, when her only responsibility was to hold a bag.

Years after high school she found undeposited checks she'd received as graduation gifts that were now null and void, simply because she forgot to take them to the bank.

That didn't hold a candle to being 22 years old and confessing to her parents that she was thousands of dollars in credit card debt, not because she didn't have the money, but because she'd lost or forgotten bills, she was paying off sky-high interest rates.

Just another reinforcement there was no system to keep track of finances, manage her life, or follow up on important items.

Now, as an adult, this woman runs a global company focused on productivity, time management, and organization. She is even audacious enough to call it by a name that announces to the world that she is large and in charge. **Life Is Organized**.

I know from personal experience that with the right training and guidance, anything is possible.

If I could go from unorganized, unsystematic, hopelessly careless (and probably in my parents' minds, praying that I married well), to streamlined, simplified, and happily "processized" ...*Is that even a word?...* - you can too!

It doesn't take fairy dust or wishing or hoping or wanting or whining or crying or believing or wondering. It takes simple steps, commitment, and consistency.

I didn't get here overnight, in a few weeks, or even in a few months. It has taken me time. Lots of it, and I'm telling you it's possible for you too. It doesn't need to take you nearly as long as it took me. My goal is to help you skip all the self-sabotaging thoughts and beliefs, get you into immediate action, and fast-track your success.

Did you notice of the "code letters" at the start of each Chapter in this book? Together they spell:

A.C.T.I.O.N.S.

Exactly the ones for you to take to focus on the things that matter most in your life, get more of the right things done, and feel happier and more accomplished along the way.

Consider this last Chapter your cheat sheet. We'll review all seven A.C.T.I.O.N.S so you, too, can look in the mirror one day and think: "Is that focused and successful person really me?"

Let's start from the beginning.

A in A.C.T.I.O.N.S.**: Avoid distractions.**

You might have a misconception about multi-tasking. That it's doing two things at the same time. Like typing an email with your left hand while responding to a text with your right. That's not what most people do. It's more like starting an email and then responding to a text 90 seconds later.

Multitasking is shifting your focus between two or more tasks within just seconds or minutes of each other. Although every thumbs up emoji or text response delivers an irresistible shot of dopamine, (that addictive reward drug), it comes at a high expense.

Multitasking costs you time. Constantly shifting between tasks is a time waster. Processing information, shifting your focus, and then reprocessing again, takes seconds and minutes each time. Over the course of the day, it easily adds up to at least a precious hour or two, or even more.

Multitasking costs you energy. Each time you disengage from a task, put your focus somewhere else, (even momentarily) and then re-engage in your task, your brain battery chips away little bits at a time. The snowball effect of energy and focus depletion, usually around 3:00 p.m. leaves you feeling fried, scattered, and left wondering, "What did I get done today?"

Multitasking costs you clarity. Sending that email without the attachment, forgetting names, general brain fog. You can blame it all on your buddy, Multi-tasking, who by the way is best friends with Distractions, and loves to hang out and suck the focus out of you.

They really are no fun.

So how do you avoid them? Here's the quickie version I promised you:

1. Clear your desk (actually take all the stickies, notebooks, papers, magazines, gum wrappers, etc. and put them behind you).

2. Close all your tabs (except for the one thing you're focusing on).

3. Turn off your notifications on your phone or computer. Seriously.

4. Put your phone on "Do not disturb" mode (there is nothing simpler and more effective).

5. Use Pomodoro's (Focus Keeper app). Yes, you CAN stay focused, if you knew it was only for 25 minutes. Take the Pomodoro challenge. You will thank us both.

Take control of your distractions and take control of your life.

Let's move on to C in A.C.T.I.O.N.S.**: Commit to your priorities.**

When you think about how you want to live your life, what exactly comes to mind? Do you see yourself traveling the world, feeling healthy, writing a book, or building your own business? However you choose to live your life will most likely be determined by how you set your priorities.

When you want to make changes to your life, it's important to know what's most valuable to you. Sometimes, though, it can be hard to figure this out when you're constantly running around, reacting, and just barely staying afloat. You start to lose focus on what you originally wanted in the first place.

Take a break. Think about your life. What is really important to you?

How would you like to live your life? Write it down.

Would you like to be healthy and vital? Write it down.

Would you like to have more fun with your family and feel the love? Write it down.

What is truly important to you, the things that three years from now will make you proud? Write them down.

Determining your priorities is the first step in making worthwhile plans and goals for your days, weeks, and months. When you think about what matters the most to you, are you spending time doing those things that really matter? Do you find yourself spending too much time on things that steal your joy and just cause you frustration?

Sometimes we can spend an entire day working so hard only to feel like we've failed at the end of the day. The truth is some things are more important than others. Every day you and I have to make choices about how we will spend our time. Everyone gets the same 24 hours a day.

Which is why falling in love with your Power Hour is your most unparalleled and highest result producing tool EVER. Your Power Hour may be the most critical hour of your business, career, relationship, and life. Yes, it is that powerful.

Your Power Hour is the first hour of your day to focus on your big priorities. I recommend, two Power Hours each day. One for your personal priorities and one for your professional priorities. Here's how your Power Hour works.

Before you do anything else (like read and respond to emails, jump into social media, get on the phone, deal with an "emergency," – Commit to your top priorities.

Hint: These are usually the things that consistently get pushed to the end of the day or inadvertently procrastinated. Those things you know you really *should* be doing but aren't. (Think sales calls, exercising, strategy, planning, writing and creating).

There are two keys to reinforcing this time actually happens:

#1: Put it on your calendar. Front and center. First thing every day. Perhaps it's blocked off on your calendar from 8:30 a.m. to 9:30 a.m. or 10:00 a.m. to 11:00 a.m. or 6:00 a.m. to 7:00 a.m. There's no hard and fast rule, other than it should be before you fall into the quicksand of your other work and get distracted. This will help reinforce this practice for you, as well as let other people who have access to your schedule, know that you are busy.

#2: Use a timer. I recommend doing two Pomodoro's during this time. That means set your Pomodoro (or Focus Keeper) app for one 25-minute session. If you need the 5-minute break to stretch, pee, get coffee, or scan (not respond to) your email, by all means, do it. As soon as you hear the "ding" move right into your second Pomodoro, and that's it. That's your Power Hour for the day.

Do those two tasks and you'll increase your Power Hour success tenfold.

Like Nike says: Just Doooo It!

Okay now that you're clear on priorities and how to make them happen let's move to T in A.C.T.I.O.N.S.: Time Block.

Ever feel like your day has flown by and all you've done is react, react, react? Between your meetings and appointments, you're incessantly responding to emails, texts, calls, and people walking in and out. It's hard to actually get the real work done, isn't it?

You jeopardize what's most important when you don't have time blocked on your calendar to work on the proposal, write the blog post, fold the laundry, edit the chapter, run the errands, update the schedule, or strategize the campaign.

On the other hand, when your time is blocked, you have a roadmap for your day. It gives you guidance on what to say yes to, what to say no to, where to put your energy and where to let it go. It allows you to respond accurately when someone asks you for coffee, a minute of your time, or simply walks into your office when you're scheduled to work on "Q1 strategy planning." It holds you accountable and stops paralysis dead in its tracks.

Instead of wasting valuable time on thinking about what you should be working on, what to focus on next, and reorganizing your to-do lists (again), you'll have a plan in place that literally tells you what to do.

Important Tip: Spend five minutes every evening blocking your calendar for the next day. In between your meetings and appointments, block out the time to get your work done on specific projects and tasks. If you're into feeling like fifty pounds have been lifted off your shoulders, you will come to love using this strategy.

Now that you're clear on avoiding distractions, committing to your priorities and time blocking, **let's mosey on over to I in** A.C.T.I.O.N.S: **Invest in help.**

If you pride yourself on doing it all yourself, remember, that mentality leads to exhaustion, inefficiency, and low productivity. Getting it all done without any help holds you back from reaching your potential and feeling awesome about yourself along the way.

This mentality can also disguise itself as an undercover procrastination tool. A way to put off doing the challenging work like hiring a new team and actually getting a plan in place to train them. Not always fun, I know, but so necessary if you want to develop, grow, and have more time for the people and things you love in your life.

In the very act of getting help, you will grow as a human, leader, manager, parent, and friend. You will unburden yourself of great anxiety and stress. You will have mental, physical, and emotional space to focus on bigger picture ideas and strategies vs. staying stuck in the mundane ones that keep your life and work at a standstill.

If you think delegating takes too much time, the truth is, you don't have time to *not* delegate. The more you get off your plate, the more time and energy you will have to focus on strategy, planning and other priorities that impact your growth.

The idea that it's easier to do this myself than to teach someone else, may be true, however, the long-term benefit of eliminating a task will always be greater than the temporary pain of teaching someone else. Once you get the support you really need, you'll wonder why it took you so long to get in the first place.

If you're open-minded and aware that perhaps everything you do your way isn't always the best way and that other people can bring fresh and exciting perspectives, you'll also learn to compromise and mold your expectations.

Invest in help, whether it be small and mighty, or big and powerful. People who accomplish more and consistently feel good about what they get done, use their time and resources in the most effective way possible. If you want to feel valued and really awesome at the end of each day, get the support you need to get you there.

Quick recap on *how* to get help and delegate:

1. <u>Match the person to the job</u>: Set your assistant up for success by being aware of matching specific skill sets or areas of growth for specific requests.

2. <u>Describe the benefit</u>: Acknowledge not only their role but also how completing this task or project will benefit them. At the end of the day, everyone wants to know, "What's in it for me?" and "Why should I care?"

3. <u>Provide clear direction:</u> Create guidelines or other documentation (video is awesome) that clearly lays out all the steps.

4. <u>Have clear results:</u> The more specific, measurable results that people can accomplish, the happier and more motivated they will be.

5. <u>Encourage participation and discussion</u>: People will be more vested in you and their results when they can count on open lines of communication and encouragement.

6. <u>Leave the person alone</u>: Nobody wants to be micromanaged.

7. <u>Appreciate and recognize:</u> Don't overlook two powerful words: "Thank You." Even when the

job doesn't go exactly as you planned. Gratitude goes a long way in job satisfaction and personal motivation.

In the words of the great author, John Maxwell, *"If you want to do a few small things right, do them yourself. If you want to do great things and make a big impact, learn to delegate."*

With A. C. T. I. under your belt, you're well on your way to a happier and more rewarding life. **Let's keep up the momentum with O in** A.C.T.I.**O.**N.S.: **Own your voice.**

The next time you accept, nod, shake on, or sign another commitment, ask yourself these three questions:

1. What else do I currently have going on?

2. Do I have the time, space, and energy to take this on (and do it well)?

3. By taking this on, will I still have the time and space I need for my big priorities?

Take the couple of minutes to process it, think it through and make an intentional decision.

The simplest way I've learned to say "no" is to communicate. People will eventually respect you for taking control of your time and needs.

Saying "no" shows you have a vision, a plan, and an opinion.

Saying "no" gives you authority.

Saying "no", shows you're in control of the situation, and that you have integrity in your personal and professional value.

It also makes you feel really, really good about yourself.

By letting people know your needs, challenges, deadlines, or other commitments, you not only begin to eliminate distractions, but you also stop feeling inclined to people please all the time.

When "no" isn't appropriate, get your point across without actually using the word. In fact, say the opposite. "Yes, I can! Let's just figure out how." With this strategy, you are always viewed as a positive team player and partner, which is a home run because nobody wants to work with Negative Nelly.

Finally, remember to use your beautiful voice to take control of meetings. With a few simple phrases, (*Just want to remind everyone we're at our halfway point...*), you can wrangle in long-winded ramblers and off-point storytellers that sabotage meetings and throw them off course. Use time language to create boundaries in all areas of your life.

Bottom Line: *Ain't nobody gonna respect your time, unless you do.*

We're nearing the end of A.C.T.I.O.**N**.S. and if you're having a hard time remembering all this you're gonna love **N: No more in your head.**

For the love of all things empowering, please stop relying on your memory. You invest vital energy in remembering, double checking and thinking about what you've might have inadvertently forgotten. Instead write, write, write. Every time you have a thought - get it down.

Your inability to keep everything straight, top-of-mind, and in order has a diminishing effect on your productivity. That's why it's critical to continuously **empty your brain.**

Get as much out of your head and as possible. That means keeping a notepad with you (or a note taking-app on your phone) at all times. Place your notepads or notebooks in areas around your home and office where you typically spend a lot of time. I'm talking at your bathroom counter, bedside table, car dashboard, coffee table, kitchen counter, purse, or back pocket. Everywhere.

There are two key steps to make the list work effectively:

#1: Break down all your projects into detailed tasks
#2: Use a verb (an action) in each of your tasks

Detailed task-based lists, although longer, are CLEAR and ACTIONABLE. Unlike the "project-based lists" it gives you direction and motivates immediate action. So, instead of feeling overwhelmed and panicked when you look at your list, you start moving forward on projects.

Lastly, use checklists to save you miles of stress, hours of time, and buckets of energy.

Checklists result in three very important benefits for your time and sanity:

- You free up mental space by not having to store all those tasks, next steps, chores, and to-do's in that precious brain of yours

- You save massive time in not having to think and re-think and remember, forget, and re-remember all "the things"

- You plummet your anxiety by avoiding thoughts like, "What was I supposed to do?" "Did I already do that?" "What's the other thing that had to get done?" etc.

Bottom line: If you think it, write it down.

You made it to the very end of A.C.T.I.O.N.S! **Let's bring this baby home with S: Systems.**

Systems are liberating. They give you the freedom of time, space, energy, serenity, and money.

There are endless opportunities to create processes and systems in your business and personal life. Everything from a morning routine, to how you invoice a client, to what you need to pack for a meeting. Pretty much every part of your day can have a system.

To make a system foolproof, you know the drill. Get the system down on paper so you're not wasting your precious energy on thinking about the process over and over again. Yes, even something you've done a hundred times like pack for a day trip, write a proposal, or prepare for a presentation.

Remember, think of your step-by-step directions like a Lego manual. Do not assume that anyone understands what is in your head or what seems obvious to you. Anybody should be able to pick up the document, follow step-by-step directions, and successfully complete it.

I'm betting you have a ton of opportunities to systemize information, processes, or foundations in your life right now. In the adult world, we call these templates.

Templates are great for emails, questions, or information you are repeatedly creating/answering. Like, how about those five or six questions you get asked about regarding your return policy or sign up process or location, over and over again? What about the contract you have to send out every time you get a new client?

Don't waste your time constantly recreating the wheel. Keep a document of templates so you're not wasting time recreating similar information. Create templates for this information in forms of an FAQ page on your website or a Commonly Asked Questions sheet you can easily email.

Email templates are one of my favorite ways to save time, respond quickly and avoid procrastinating to write them. I have templates for when I'm introducing myself to someone new, reaching out for a speaking engagement, thanking someone after a conversation, following up about an order, providing next steps for coaching, training requirements, and many more.

Lastly, try Batching.

The idea of batching means to do a set of similar tasks at one time, rather than spreading smaller jobs over a number of days. It saves time in retrieving and putting away supplies and helps keep you focused on one task only. Batching will help you remain consistent with your organization. Group similar work into batches. Batching allows you to stay more focused, feel less scattered, and be more efficient with your time.

Bottom line: Systems rule. The more you have them in your life (even you creative folk) the more in control and happier you'll be.

So, there you have it. All seven **A.C.T.I.O.N.**S. to get you rollin' in the control zone and feeling accomplished every. single. day.

You're either thinking, "Are you kidding me? That's a lot!" or "This all sounds so good, I can't wait to jump in on every single last strategy."

Perhaps you're somewhere in the middle, ready to thumb back to a particular Chapter or two to reinforce the ideas that really hit home for you.

Here's the deal. If you've made it this far into the book, you are a high achiever. I know you high achieving types (takes one to know one) and you're excited to improve your circumstances and grow your skills. Given that, I don't want this to be a book that you're:

A. Pumped about but don't take action

B. Excited about and take action on six different things

C. Collects dust as you start reading your next book from your pile

Having worked with hundreds of awesome people I'll share two things I've learned about successfully adopting new habits and behaviors.

Numero uno: You need to work on ONE habit at a time. Only one. Start, practice, get better, master it, then move on to the next.

Numero dos: You need accountability. Not just to yourself because if you're anything like me, you're the easiest person to let down.

In order to start one habit at a time, think about the seven habits in taking new A.C.T.I.O.N.S. Chances are there was ONE that really resonated with you. One that made you think,

"I have got to stop (or start) doing this!"

"This is so me!"

"This will make all the difference!"

If you had that moment more than once, think again, and for the love of all things simple and that really work, pick ONE strategy you'll commit to. Here's the cheat sheet again.

A: Avoid distractions

C: Commit to your priorities

T: Time block

I: Invest in help

O: Own your voice

N: No more in your head!

S: Systemize

I've armed you with tips and tools within each of these strategies so even when you pick ONE ... *Which you already have, right?* you'll have plenty of support in that chapter to make it work.

Just like uni-tasking (remember that idea from avoiding distractions?) staying focused on one habit change at a time is your key to success. When you try to make several changes at the same time, you might be successful for a few days, or in some cases a few hours, but chances are they'll all fall by the wayside sooner rather than later.

Instead, pick one, put it into use, test it, tweak it, try it, fail at it, try it again, succeed at it, and then wake up tomorrow morning and do it all over again. It's a habit. You don't learn to block your time and stop multitasking or avoid distractions in one try or one day. You keep at it, day after day, hour after hour, until you catch yourself NOT doing it. Then you simply give yourself the GRACE you deserve and push yourself to get back on the bandwagon and do it again.

It's like eating healthy or getting more exercise. You want to get to the point where you feel like crap when you don't do it consistently. That simply means you recognize its benefits and are well on your way to habit mode.

Then, my sweet friend, focus on another strategy that speaks to you. Which means your next actions might look something like this:

You recognize that C: Committing to your priorities is where you'll benefit most. Your sales are less than lackluster, and you need to get focused on them, pronto. So, you go through the exercise of scheduling your Power Hour every day through the week. Reality hits and given all your meetings and appointments (that can't be changed at this point) you can only dedicate thirty minutes on Wednesday and forty minutes on Friday. Instead of blowing it off, you schedule that time and vow to not respond to email until after you're done each day. Some days are successful. Others are not.

You don't beat yourself up over it but recognize what you need to tweak the following week to ensure more success. Like, you need to wake up 45 minutes earlier the days you want to workout AND get your Power Hour in before 9:00 a.m. You do it one day and hit snooze the next. The next week, you tweak strategies, and you implement it again. By this point you are absolutely seeing and feeling the benefits of committing to this time, in fact, you made one new sale and have three very qualified prospects to follow up with. Now that you're beginning to make your power hour a habit, perhaps it's time to implement another strategy, like adding Systems to your prospecting, sales, and follow up tasks.

See how it works? Test one strategy, use it, tweak it, fall off, get back on, start creating the habit, then move onto strategy #2 (while continuing to use strategy #1).

This will be the difference between reading this book, taking action, failing, and thinking "nothing ever works for me" and reading this book, taking action, succeeding, and thinking, "Yes! I finally found something that works for me."

Failure usually doesn't lie in the strategy. It lies in the execution.

So, in my usual, I will beat-you-over-the-head about it fashion, commit to ONE of the A.C.T.I.O.N.S. and go full throttle on it before putting another into effect. *Kapeesh?* Cool.

Remember the second success strategy I mentioned earlier in this Chapter? Accountability. You need it. Not just to yourself but to someone else. Putting your goals out into the world (and beyond your mind) makes them real and actionable.

So, #2, once you've committed to one of the seven strategies, hold yourself accountable by letting me know which one it is. Email me at **mridu@lifeisorganized**. I read and respond to every email. If you are serious about taking control of your time and life, you'll take this step and let me cheer you on and help you make it happen.

This brings us to the end of our journey together.

I remember back in the day when I was dealing with my failing business and feeling disconnected from my family. Overwhelmed and overworked, I didn't have much to show for all my efforts, and I knew it would take me years and years to reach my goals.

I realized that I wasn't someone who treated her time with the respect it deserved. I was snugly curled up in my comfort zone, doing the easy things, the distracting things, the things that kept me busy, busy, busy. It wasn't the truly important stuff, the right stuff, or the things that mattered most to me.

What about now? With simple changes in my schedule, shutting out time wasters, and getting systems in place I've transformed my life from confusion and chaos to clarity and confidence.

I want to leave you with this.

Instead of getting caught up in the drama and your feelings of overwhelm, see these limiting beliefs as what they are...make believe and more importantly, within your control. You possess the mindset, tools, and strategies to take control of them.

The difference between you feeling frenetic and embracing composure is your decision to be in the driver's seat. Of course, it can be terrifying to do things differently, but when you commit to managing your life in a meaningful way, you will be and feel more successful than ever.

When you get control of your time you can do anything. You can reach any goal you want. You can become the coach, write the book, lose the weight, get the promotion, build the house, find the guy, start the foundation, and create the memories.

You will be more focused, more confident, more successful, and happier than ever before.

If you want to take control of your time, take control of your time. Get out of your own way.

Imagine how awesome it's going to feel when you get the important things done. When you go to bed feeling accomplished night after night. When you defy a lifetime's worth of lies about your ability to succeed and reach your goals.

Imagine when you and time and goals are besties, in control of your own destiny and results.

Imagine how rewarding your life will be when you consistently accomplish what you set out to do.

So, go out there, friend.

Honor your commitments.

Respect your time.

Embrace your journey.

Finally, get the right things done.